City Hall and Mrs. God
a passionate journey through a changing toronto

City Hall
& Mrs. God

*a passionate journey
through a changing Toronto*

Cary Fagan

THE MERCURY PRESS
(AN IMPRINT OF AYA PRESS)
Stratford, Ontario

The publisher gratefully acknowledges the financial assistance of the Canada Council and the Ontario Arts Council.

ACKNOWLEDGEMENTS:

The author would like to thank all those who spoke to him.
Also, Beverley and Don Daurio for their encouragement.
And the Ontario Arts Council for a Writers' Reserve grant.

Among the sources for historical information about Toronto, the author would like to acknowledge particularly the following: *Toronto to 1918*, by J.M.S. Careless; *Toronto since 1918* by James Lemon; *Spadina Avenue* by Rosemary Donegan and Rick Salutin; and *Toronto Architecture: a City Guide*, by Patricia McHugh.

Lines from "A History of Vietnam and Central America..." from *Furious*, by Erin Mouré. Used by permission, Stoddart Publishing Company Limited.

Events in this book took place between March and September, 1989.
A few of the names have been changed.

Cover design: Scott McKowen
Production co-ordination and page design: The Blue Pencil
Typography: The Beacon Herald, Stratford, Ontario.
Printed and bound at Hignell Printing, Winnipeg.

Canadian Cataloguing in Publication:

Fagan, Cary.
City hall & Mrs. God: a passionate journey through a changing Toronto

ISBN 0-920544-73-8

1. Toronto (Ont.) - Social conditions. 2. Social structure - Ontario - Toronto.   I. Title.

HN110.T6F3 1990   971.3'541   C90-094039-5

Sales Representation: The Literary Press Group.

The Mercury Press is distributed in Canada by University of Toronto Press, and in the United States by Inland Book Company (selected titles) and Bookslinger.

The Mercury Press
(an imprint of Aya Press)
Box 446
Stratford, Ontario
Canada
N5A 6T3

CONTENTS

A Beginning 7

Incoherence 10

The Five Hundred Dollar Pig 24

Cheap Entertainment 40

Schmoozing 49

Mrs. God's Wounds 70

Jaguars 93

The Miss Toronto Pageant 109

Singers on a Bus 132

A Beginning

ON THE STAGE of Lee's Palace a band called Skull Valley is playing straight-up rock and roll. Beyond the bar where I lean is the pit for a dance floor. The darkness pierced by strobes, the pounding beat, the movement of bodies is strangely soothing so late at night. Closing my eyes, with the cold bottle of beer against my forehead, I am swimming through the ocean, or rather turning endlessly round and round, running out of air. Toronto has changed in the two years I've been away, changed so obviously that at certain moments it feels like a different city. Walking downtown I hardly recognize some blocks, so many new towers have gone up with their polished facades and glassed-in atriums. And the crowds, on the sidewalks and in the subways, are denser than before and the greater diversity of faces— black, white, Asian, Spanish— would be cause for celebration were it not for the crushing sense of impatience and anger.

None of Toronto's problems are a secret. The people who live here feel them every day; there is talk of "Manhattanization," of a city beginning to reel out of control, grown too large for anyone to really know what is going on. Even the press is screaming. The local CBC ran a series called "The Price of Prosperity," the *Toronto Star* published a run of special reports, the *Globe & Mail* detailed the influence of developers on local councillors. But many of these stories feed on people's fears and none of them has given me a sense of what is really happening in the city.

And so I swim. Unsure of which way is up or down. Returning to Toronto, I saw that it had grown in ways that as a lover of cities I appreciated. The street cafés are buzzing, the small theatres take risks and thrive, people dress with more quirky individuality. Posters for dances and demonstrations cover the street poles and hoardings faster than the efficient army of cleaners can tear them down. These are not mere diversions, but signs of a city's pulse, its heart-beat. On a subway platform I saw a large black woman, maybe two hundred and fifty pounds, dancing to the sound of her Walkman. She looked *good*. As for the old, some of the places that I like best— such as College Street, where my grandfather had his first leather factory— are still much the same. So much is worth saving.

But some people are moving out of Toronto, to Stratford or Kingston or Vancouver, squeezed out by housing prices or just fed up with frenzy and greed. What surprises me most is how little regret they feel, the absence of any loyalty to Toronto. Perhaps it is because this city, unlike New York or Montreal, has created no myth of itself to hold them. But these are people who have a choice, who can leave if they want to. Some are moving so that they can own their own homes one day; others, by selling the houses they do own, are departing with a tidy windfall. For it is the paradox of an economic boom and surge of new money that has changed Toronto for the worse.

Commerce made Toronto. It was founded in the eighteenth century for trade, a means rather than an end, a place connected to other places by water, road, and then rail. Poverty has always increased here in bad times and subsided in good— wealth in Toronto meant better times for everyone. Now, while the wealth has become obvious, so has the poverty. And just as obvious is the conspicuous consumption, as if people in Toronto have lost that historic sense of English reticence. Lost it not to dance on subway platforms, but to cruise up to Creeds in shark-like limousines, pay for thousand-dollar-a-ticket opera balls, and line up at Bemelmans and Brownes.

When I first decided to write this book, a friend gave me a copy of V.S. Naipaul's *A Turn in the South*, the account of his tour of the southern United States. What struck me was that Naipaul had no stake in the place he explored; after writing the book he would leave again, never to return. Because of that he was free to say whatever he wanted, but at the same time it seemed to matter less. Toronto is my home and it seems not good enough to take a distanced and supposedly objective view. I want to use this book for my own purposes, to turn it into a doorway through which I can enter the life of the city in a way that I never have before and that I suspect most people never do. Toronto people lead obsessively private lives, rarely if ever engaging in public activity, making their voices heard, trying to affect the city they live in. That is why, much as I admire George Orwell's *Down and Out in Paris and London*, I have decided not to put on the rags of a beggar, or even a tuxedo for that matter, and take on an undercover existence. Instead, I will simply be myself. That way whatever I learn I will take back with me into my real life, rather than shedding it afterwards like a suit of clothes.

The band is really driving now and in the pit below two women are dancing, not together but alone. To write about a city is to tame its mystery and beauty, to remove its claws and teeth of cruelty. But how can you tame something that is always changing, creating a dozen secrets for every one that it gives up? The bottle of beer has gone warm. On stage the band's singer, wearing a white T-shirt and jeans like Bruce Springsteen, pounds on his beautiful black guitar and sings—

We don't believe there's redemption of souls,
we don't believe because we are the dead men—

Incoherence

FROM THE THREE NARROW neo-gothic windows the sky is as dark as blue can be and beyond the shapes of the university rise the distant towers of the financial district, illuminated like modernist sculptures. From somewhere in the building— in Hart House— comes the sound of a student band practicing swing tunes. For a moment it seems like war-time: students crossing the darkened campus during a dim-out, new recruits bedding down in the horse stalls of the Exhibition. It was the war that chased my own father, barely a teenager, out of Europe and eventually to this university.

The view from the library window is one of my favourites in the city. The room itself is all arches, red plush and plaster faces of lions, and was built at a time when Toronto looked to England for its standards and prejudices. But the city did begin to accept outsiders in its stand-offish way, even if in limited numbers. Now, standing by the open window, I can smell Toronto, a cool city smell, and hear the roll of distant traffic. It is a view that makes me sentimental and vaguely happy and reminds me how much I love the city I was born to.

While I stand in reflection something brushes against me, and as I move aside a figure passes, muttering, and climbs onto the narrow window-bench. The figure, dressed in a dirty blazer, dingy white pants, and oversized men's shoes without socks, stretches out as best it can and then, turning its head, looks at me. The figure is a woman, with a face so creased from exposure and hair so matted that her age is indeterminable. A black discoloration runs along her cheekbone. She looks at me for three or four seconds and I cannot read her eyes. And then she turns away and, using a book as a pillow, appears to go to sleep.

Over her body, I can still see the view through the windows— the blue-black sky, the glinting Royal Bank Tower. But it isn't the same. The pleasure is gone but I cannot turn away immediately. For a moment I feel a surprising anger at this— this person for having ruined the moment. Then the anger subsides and is replaced by a desire to imagine what it is like to lie on that bench, with someone staring at my back while I try to sleep. But here my imagination fails.

From somewhere in the building comes the sound of enthusiastic applause.

AT THE FRONT of the meeting room in the John Innis Community Centre on Sherbourne Street there is a display of boards illustrating the proposed Cathedral Square condominium project. I first saw these boards, along with a pretty scale model, at the Condominium Living Show, held in the vast and sterile space of the Convention Centre. There all the developers' displays boasted of design and location, and listed such similar luxuries that they began to seem as standard as kitchen sinks: hot tubs and microwaves, private patios and marble bathroom countertops. The names of the buildings were rather desperate attempts to capture the glamour of anywhere but the city where they will stand: the Memphis, the Ellington, the Empire Plaza. Not long after, I received a card in the mail for a new development called Le Metropole, with a make-believe address in Paris.

"That thing?" the young black man next to me says, wrinkling up his nose at the illustration of Cathedral Square. "Put that up where the Terrace is? No way." The room in the community centre fills up with people who have come for the public hearing on the rezoning of the Terrace site at Dundas and Victoria streets. Like me, most of them have never been to a hearing before. The design for Cathedral Square is of a high, ornate yellow building with rounded corners and intricate railings. It looks like something from Florida or New Orleans rather than Toronto, and when I first saw it I thought the

11

building unusual and perhaps even attractive. But these people obviously feel differently. They want the Terrace, Toronto's only roller-skating rink and the original home of the Maple Leafs, to stay open. But the Dixon family has already sold it to the Centara Corporation, which has shut down the rink while waiting for zoning approval.

As the meeting gets underway, David Smith, the developer's lawyer begins to speak. A square man with wavy hair, he is a former city councillor and notorious for his persuasive skills. Smith praises the crowd for its efforts at keeping roller skating alive in the city and says that due to the efforts of councillor Jack Layton all the equipment from the rink will be donated to the city. As a sign of good will, the developer won't knock down the Terrace until the zoning is approved, despite having obtained a demolition permit.

Hissing from the crowd.

Jack Layton gets up. He wears a white shirt over his muscular chest and the trademark red suspenders. Layton is the New Democratic Party member leading the so-called reformers who have gained power in the last election, sweeping out many of the pro-development old guard. He's a handsome and charismatic man with a flat but powerful speaking voice. It wasn't him who has gone this far to preserve the rink, he declares, but the people in this very room.

Thunderous applause.

The architect of Cathedral Square rises, a thin and dour man in a double breasted suit named Richard Young from the firm of Young and Wright. Taking from his pocket a retractable pointer, he begins to explain the design in a manner more appropriate for potential investors than a hostile crowd. The centre building will rise seventeen stories next to a second of thirteen, with a separate block of assisted housing to be built by the city. The developer's giving up a corner of land for the city building is one of the sweeteners by which it hopes to get the increased zoning approved.

A young man in a short-sleeved shirt calls out in an angry voice, "The flip charts are all very nice. And the building's very nice. But none of us are going to live in it, so what is the point of all this detail?"

People applaud. A woman shouts, "This meeting is going on too long. How about people who have children to get home to?" But the architect seems incapable of abridging his presentation. He points to the underground-parking entrance, highlights what he calls the "detailed fenestration." A young blond woman rises from her chair. She is wearing a T-shirt decorated with an illustration of a man standing before a tank in Tiananmen Square. "First of all," she says, "I think it's the ugliest building I've ever seen." Tremendous applause. "It doesn't fit into the neighbourhood." That is simple and true— I hadn't considered it. The woman says how offensive it is that the socially-assisted housing is "segregated" from the condominium.

David Smith continues calmly. He says that the developer has been impressed by the enthusiasm and concern of these young people. A man jumps up. "I don't think the developer is impressed. I don't think the developer's kids go to the roller skating rink. They go to Switzerland for the summer."

Laughter. The separation between the two sides has grown wider; an appalling sense of rich and poor has seeped into the room. David Smith, dropping his diplomatic tone, says, "I think you should understand that the owning of property brings with it certain rights."

A man stands up, of fifty or more, with thick glasses and bad teeth. He chokes on his words with such grief or anger that he can hardly get them out and the audience strains to hear. "A woman... got frozen... to death trying to get into the... building." He's almost weeping. Two homeless people, Jack Layton explains, have died in the doorway of a boarded-up building on Shuter Street that is owned by the RCMP.

"You're condo-ing us to death!" shouts a female voice. More cheers. Somebody asks sarcastically about Cathedral Square's recreational facilities. The architect uses his retractable pointer to indicate the swimming pool and squash courts. A voice asks innocently: "I was wondering, these squash courts, are they going to be for the social-housing tenants too?" What laughter! People are shaking in their seats around me.

A boy of thirteen or so gets up. "This thing is totally unnecessary," he says. "I have a lot of friends. We like to go out after doing our homework, not to break windows but to have fun. If we go to the Eaton Centre the cops think we're trying to steal something. Where are we going to go now?"

"This isn't a people place, it's a concrete jungle," somebody shouts. "We're saying it's not a city for youth, it's not a city for the working Joe."

"The city is turning its back on its children!"

Jack Layton, sensing that the meeting has come to a head, gets up. When he talks he stands like a boxer, feet firmly planted, fists almost punching the air. "Twenty million dollars extra could be found to open the Skydome on time," he says. "That's enough to build three roller-skating rinks. I'd like the owners of Cathedral Square to identify themselves. I'd like to look them straight in the face. If anyone tries to tear that building down they're going to have to call the cops because I and a lot of other people will be there!"

Wild cheering. It is past ten-thirty; the meeting has gone on for over three hours. Layton speaks more calmly now, trying to conciliate. But the anger in the room throbs like a heart in a fist. These people are mad, and not just about the Terrace but about what's happening to the city that no longer seems theirs. Sitting in my chair, I envy their emotion and wish I could join in. But I am outside, a dispassionate observer, an emotional voyeur. Three young men in suits sitting in the last row are the only others not cheering. Just as the meeting ends they smile to one another and slip out the back.

ON BLOOR STREET a person can walk from St. George to Bathurst and be accosted by four, five, even six beggars, hands outstretched. Young men with earrings, girls with orange hair, old women surrounded by shopping bags, sad-looking drunks. Their approaches are modest, aggressive, amused, indifferent, anguished; and their number is astounding, four or five times as many as just a couple of years ago. As I pass each one I go through the same excruciating socio-moral-political arguments for giving money to strangers. Does it help, or contribute to the problem? Will the money be used for drugs or drink? Doesn't the person have a right to find his solace any way he can? Am I being made a fool of? With each new hand the arguments grow only more impossible.

Now, in the late afternoon, a native woman and two native men are sitting on the step of a discount clothing store at Palmerston.

From one to another they pass a plastic grocery bag with its rim rolled down and each in turn holds the bag to his mouth and takes in deep breaths. One of the men, a big fellow with long and greasy hair, rises unsteadily to his feet. He holds out his hand but people hurry past and he half turns to follow them, wobbling precariously. In frustration he reaches out, grasps a woman by the wrist, and slurs something about money. "Don't touch me," the woman says, and pulls away. He tries to ask several more but they pass so quickly he is almost whirled in a circle. Finally he grabs hold of a man in a windbreaker. The two scuffle, the man throws a punch into the native man's face, and a rack of handbags goes flying.

Next to me a young man with a shaved head turns and grins. "The Indians are on the warpath," he says.

EARLY FOR MY MEETING with Parika, I walk across Oak Street, the central road of Regent Park North that is closed to traffic. Although I have often gone by Regent Park (I remember thinking as a child how gloomy the low, box-like buildings were) I have never before been in it. Like so many people, I am a stranger in my own city, unaware of how the days pass for people whose lives are different from my own. And like many I have a mild distaste, perhaps even a fear, for what I don't know.

Regent Park is the country's oldest and biggest public-housing project, built in 1947 when planners and politicians believed that the way to help the poor was to reorder the spaces of their lives, to knock down neighbourhoods and put up neat and orderly projects. The buildings off Oak Street are three or six stories high, built of dull red brick in Corbusier's cruciform plan. Everybody knows such plans are a mistake now, but their legacy lives on as the east end still contains the greatest concentration of assisted housing and social agencies. The drabness and uniformity, the blank worn spaces between buildings where debris shifts and glass shards glint— it all freezes the heart. Perhaps it's also this grey day threatening rain, but the feeling is desolate and I feel a depression seeping through me like a chill.

A few mothers with their kids are sitting on folding chairs in the doorway of one of the apartments. In front of the recreation building a girl is seriously petting her dog, while closer to River Street two boys are playing with discarded boards of insulation. I don't cross the murky water of the Don River, but turn back towards the United Church near Parliament Street where I'm supposed to meet Parika.

I first spoke to Parika at the Terrace hearing, and after I told her of wanting to see for myself how Toronto is changing, she offered to take me to a meeting of a group called the Roomers Association. Roomers, one of the anti-poverty groups organized at the Christian Resource Centre, was formed to improve the rights and living conditions for people who live in rooming houses.

The Christian Resource Centre (or CRC) is housed in an extension to the church in Regent Park, both of which were built on the site of a Victorian church that planners considered inappropriate to the neighbourhood and tore down. The weedy lawn doesn't look very comfortable but two men are sleeping on it anyway. Parika waits for me by the door, calling out a cheerful greeting, a shopping-bag of toilet paper in one hand. Though Parika is from Guyana, she looks and sounds East Indian to me and she tells me that some of her ancestry is Indian. She is a short woman, her jet-black hair pulled back into a braid, and with a slightly drooping eyelid. The eyelid, she says, is the result of a botched operation, and it makes her feel self-conscious, so much so that she filed a complaint against the doctor. The complaint was dismissed.

Parika needs to swear an affidavit, so we begin walking to the storefront legal clinic on Queen Street. Along the way she brings up a dozen issues, so many in fact that I can't keep up, and am amazed at how well-informed she is on city hall politics, the voting habits of councillors, and issues surrounding the poor. For a year, Parika tells me, she was a homeless person, shifting from one hostel to another. For a year now she has had permanent shelter again, but Parika tells me that "a year of having a home isn't equivalent to a year of homelessness." The mind degenerates when you don't have a place to stay, you stop taking care of yourself and the bureaucratic red-tape necessary to get help starts to defeat you. "That's why I'm incoherent," she says, and it's strangely true, for despite her lively intelligence and her clear articulation of minute details on such issues as how the Human Rights Commission disciminates against single people, I sometimes find myself unable to follow her. Inside the legal clinic, the secretary tells Parika that affidavits are sworn only until three o'clock. "Shoot, I missed it again, I am going to be in big trouble," she says. Apparently, Parika got annoyed by all the forms required by welfare and because she didn't bother to fill them out, she now must have an affidavit to prove that she has no income. Presently she is living on money that she earned during a year-long compulsory training program that she began immediately after finding shelter. The program was useless; Parika spent her time at a drop-in answering the telephone. "I have no marketable skills," she complains. "The welfare department, they want you to start looking for work as soon as you get off the streets. They don't care about your psychological problems. Everybody wants to work, why wouldn't they? But after you have a home again you are under a barrage of stimuli, you can't take it. You need time."

"I came to Canada in 1970," she says as we walk along Dundas Street towards her apartment. "With my cousin, to enter post-secondary school. Back then it was quite easy to get in, the government almost begged us. But coming here, I found it very difficult. Back home you wore one set of clothes all year round. There we had a house and could open the windows, make as much noise as we wanted, but here the floors are so squeaky and the tenants complain, and the apartments are so small. I didn't adjust. My cousin, oh she did well, she went to George Brown and got A's. The people who get A's are all cheaters, they're not honest people, that's the only way to be successful in this system. The people you see on the street, they're honest people, that's why they're there. I dropped out and went to work. I took different factory jobs, thinking that I could get a work history and end up at some place like Bell. But it doesn't work that way, and I couldn't stand the monotony. But becoming homeless doesn't happen all at once, it's gradual. Once, when I was homeless, I saw my cousin in the street. She works in a lab. She hugged me and took me home to her house for dinner. She asked me if I would come to a party that she and her husband were giving. But she told me I had to wear proper clothes or else I would embarrass them. Can you believe that? My relatives, they don't want to know me. They give me a few dollars and tell me how hard it is to make a living. That's why I don't want you to use my real name. It will embarrass them if they see it."

As Parika wants to change for the Roomers meeting, we stop at her apartment in the non-profit housing built next to All Saints Church at Dundas and Sherbourne. Her place is a mess, she says, asking me to wait outside. "I don't have furniture, except for a cot that the church gave me. I don't need furniture. Immigrants who are poor, they'll sleep on the floor or in the bathtub and it's all right, even though the social workers tell you not to."

Waiting on the sidewalk, I watch people drift in and out of the Friendship Centre, a drop-in next door. Across the road stands a Victorian house, its green paint flaking. Scribbled on the boarded-up door are the words

THIS
WAS
HOME
FOR
MANY

and underneath are signatures: *Rob, Steve, Leea-na, Cory, Simone, Mad Dog, Mike, Terry, Jackie #1 Skid*, and *Joanne #1 Prego*. On one boarded window is written *Why? Profits befor People* (sic), and on another, *Why must we suffer while you government boys get rich?*

Parika emerges again, looking neat in a turtle-neck and grey blazer. We head back to the church, where some of the Roomers members have gathered on the grass. Not long ago the group claimed a victory when the landlord and tenant laws were made to apply to rooming houses, giving roomers greater protection from rent hikes and eviction.

The members get up and go down into the basement of the Christian Resource Centre to sit in the dim light at long tables. Outside, some boys are bouncing a tennis ball against one of the windows. Michael Shapcott, a community worker behind much of the CRC's recent work, arrives from his office upstairs. He's a round-faced, round-stomached guy with a twinkling eye and when he enters the dingy basement the meeting seems to spark into sudden purpose.

Michael tells the group about an upcoming general meeting. A male voice from the rear cracks, "Is there a dress code?"

"Yes," Michael snaps back, "you've got to wear a dress. And shave your legs. That way they can't say we have no class."

Two other CRC workers attend the meeting: Carmel Hili, a soft-spoken, former Jesuit priest, and Tammie Mayes, a young woman on a grant program whom I recognize as the one at the Terrace meeting who wore the Beijing massacre T-shirt. All three give a series of reports which the eighteen Roomers members listen to with various levels of interest. Most say nothing, some make the occasional joke, and a few, like Parika, respond seriously to the issues. The group's most pressing problem is that its most active organizer, a man called Tex, has had to drop out because of a new baby. A woman near the back takes a drag on her cigarette and says, "At least he's a father who owns up."

The most vocal discussion of the evening centres on the food bank that ends every Roomers meeting, when plastic bags are given out and members line up at the tables stacked with cans of fruit and bags of bread. Some people are showing up near the end of meetings just so they can take from the food bank and often they hog the best items. How can the Roomers make sure distribution is fair?

Somebody suggests filling the bags before each meeting. Michael doesn't like the idea— too much like giving out "goodie bags" to kids rather than letting everyone choose for himself. The young man sitting next to me makes a suggestion. A newcomer to Roomers, he has a narrow face and hooded eyes. "I was just down in San Francisco," he says insouciantly, flicking his cigarette over one of the bent tuna tins used as ash trays. "And for their food banks everybody gets issued ID cards with photographs."

Tammie doesn't like that idea. "You people have to jump through too many hoops as it is," she says. She and the other workers are eager to keep the system open, democratic, and based on mutual trust, but the Roomers themselves don't seem nearly as concerned about such principles and the discussion fades away without a decision.

The young man with the dark eyes turns to me and says, "You want to know how many cop shops I've had run-ins with? The Metro

Toronto Police, the RCMP, American immigration... "He's holding a pamphlet that has been circulating during the meeting called UTOPIA IS NOW POSSIBLE. "I'm not a communist. My parents were communists, that's why they were kidnapped in Argentina and killed." His voice is bragging; I have no idea whether he is telling the truth. Parika says, "I don't believe in communism but they have some interesting things to say. Sometimes I go to the discussions at the Pathfinder Book Store. They're more open to ideas than the NDP. Interesting subjects come out."

Carmel Hili reminds the group of their plan to go to Camp Scugog in Muskoka for a weekend holiday. This is a chance to get out of Toronto, to look back on the past year and forward to new plans, but the group has been slow on deciding on a date. The last one proposed comes too close to the end of the month, when people at the camp would begin to worry about their government cheques arriving. Although the discussion has been going on for four months now no new date is arrived at.

Tammie Mayes reports on the public hearing on Cathedral Square and the efforts to save the Terrace. The Community workers wish to bring to the Roomers group many issues that don't affect them directly, to widen their political interests. But nobody but Parika seems particularly interested in roller skating. One native man with a bulbous nose says in a loud voice, "What's the difference if these rich kids have to go to Burlington in their Ferraris and Jags to roller skate?" Tammie, not wishing to lecture, disagrees and moves on. But the man speaks out again, "Last year we passed a whole list of resolutions and not one of them was done. We haven't done anything but talk."

Carmel disagrees politely but the man says, "I've passed the age of pipe dreams."

"I always have optimism," Carmel says quietly.

ON WEEKENDS the two baseball diamonds in Christie Pits are in constant use by pick-up teams of men and women and organized leagues where the local hardware store's name is emblazoned on brilliant uniforms. Today it's little league and behind the fence one of the mothers is announcing the batting line-up on a miniature p.a. system.

Christie Pits is a grassy bowl in the west end, a soft encircling cradle that holds off the moving traffic of Bloor Street below. At this time of day, it's hard to believe that drug deals are made here after the sun goes down. A tiny boy on a tiny bicycle is peddling furiously along a path, past some men playing soccer and shouting to one another in Arabic. By the volleyball court, a small crowd has stopped to watch the game, including a teenager pushing an ice-cream cart.

I sit down on a bench. Over fifty years ago, in 1933, a large crowd gathered on the opposite slope to watch a quarter-final baseball game between Harbord Playground and St. Peter's. At the end of the game a home-made flag with a swastika painted on it was unfurled in a section of the crowd. When the Jews rushed to pull it down, a riot broke out. As the word spread, Jewish and Italian boys down on College Street piled into chicken trucks and roared up to the park. They fought on the grass, on Christie and on Clinton Streets. They battled with fists, broom handles, bricks, lead pipes.

There's no memory of that night here, not in this city without a memory. Nor of the day in 1875 when Toronto Orangemen attacked a Catholic street procession. Nor of the order decreed by the mayor that once forbade any Chinese businessman from hiring a white female. There is a saying that without memory there is no past, and without past no identity. But looking about Christie Pits now, it's easy to believe that Toronto has become a more diverse and accepting city. Before my bench a young black couple walks slowly along the path, the woman carrying a near new-born in her arms. Beside the water fountain a Spanish-speaking family has finished a picnic, and to the daughter's shrieking delight, as she and her mother turn the rope, the father skips madly in the middle, throwing up his feet with surprising grace.

But some believe that the increasing pressures of the city have made intolerance flare up, and I have come to this bench to sort out two incidents from the last couple of days.

The first took place in Trinity-St. Paul's Church on Bloor Street. The chapel was appealingly dowdy and the people going inside were in a holiday mood. Kids ran down the aisles, English-language teachers greeted their adult students from South America and Hong

Kong. This was the Toronto Board of Education's Tenth Anniversary Anti-Racist Revue. On stage the rows of kids waving to their friends looked like a miniature United Nations. Each in turn came up to the microphone and how strange it was to hear them speak of "the bloodshed of the African people" and "the struggle for freedom and equality around the world." When I was in school at that age we were still tracing the route of Jacques Cartier. One girl took the microphone to talk about "biased textbooks." Kids recited poems to Martin Luther King. A class spoke of their Amnesty International Project and how they played "a simulation game about power." And then a band from Essex Public School called One World Pan played Amazing Grace on the steel drums. It sounded a bit weird but somehow right and as I listened a rush of good feeling came over me.

The second incident took place this morning, on a subway car pulling out of Sherbourne Station. A man, a woman, and a boy of about six got on and the woman sat down while the man stood in the doorway. The woman was plain and the boy homely, with a blond rat-tail at the back of his hair. When the boy tried to get up from his seat his mother said, "I'll hit you with the back of my hand," and making a sudden rush, caused him to flinch painfully. "That's the one thing you've yet to learn, Tommy," she said. "Discretion." And then she laughed, cried, "I've got your nose!" and kissed him.

The man in the doorway, who was very big, wore an Australian bush hat and enormous white shoes. He looked down at the woman and made clucking noises with his tongue, apparently a sign of affection. She looked up with a soft and yearning face. Then the man turned his head and in a low insistent voice, muttered, "You scum, you fucking Paki, you refugee— " He was speaking to a figure across the aisle, a dark-skinned and meek looking man. The man did not look up, nor did the three or four others in the car. "You fucking scum, you dirty Paki," the big man went on and on obsessively, the words like bullets. He paused only to cluck at the woman before turning back and continuing, "You fucking Paki, you scum... "

At Ossington I got off, angry and disgusted and ashamed. Perhaps if I had stayed on until this perverse nuclear family had left, I could have said to the man, "I'm sorry people in the city can behave this way, I'm sorry I did nothing... "

At the Anti-Racist Revue, I had picked up a magazine published by the students of Regal Road Public School. One page of the magazine was a blank cartoon strip that the reader was invited to fill in with this suggestion: "Design a cartoon showing a negative schoolyard incident." In the last panel of the cartoon the instruction was to draw a scene in which the incident is happily and peacefully resolved.

The question is, which image should I use to fill the last panel of the cartoon? The kids on stage, their voices singing "Go Down Moses"? Or the man in the bush hat, uttering his hate?

In the park, a bracelet of kids is going down the slide. "I was so scared," says one of them, "I forgot to scream."

The Five Hundred Dollar Pig

THIRTEEN WOMEN are standing about the basement room or sitting in the assortment of wooden stacking chairs, 1960s armchairs, pews, and if you count the not-yet-borns inside them, the number in the room almost doubles. All the stages are evident, women still slim and women with flushed faces sunk into chairs to rest their rounding bellies. Most are silent as they take slices of watermelon and apple from the trays on the long tables; only a cluster of four Spanish-speaking women are talking spiritedly. On the table a few carnations sprout from an old mayonnaise jar. A black woman walks her baby up and down the room while an Indian woman nuzzles her swaddled up, amazingly miniature newborn. A couple of kids are old enough to play with the rocking-horse or the carton of building blocks, but they cling to mothers' legs instead.

"Lisa!" a man calls from behind the counter and a woman gets up to receive her two bags of food.

Healthy Beginnings is a new program held every Wednesday by the Stop 103 food bank in the basement of this Ossington Avenue church. It is intended to reach isolated women whose pregnancies are high-risk simply because they are poor. More babies of low-income women are born underweight, have a susceptibility to illness, and die in infancy. And women, especially with children, are becoming increasingly vulnerable to poverty in the city. Healthy Beginnings is a special food bank dispensing products that other food banks don't, like fruit and cheese and milk, and gives the mothers-to-be a chance to consult with a nutritionist and a nurse. After their babies are born, the women can keep coming for six months to ensure that their own better nutrition will get passed on through the nursing milk.

But there is another goal to Healthy Beginnings and this one appears less successful and harder to achieve. Because so many of these women don't have the support groups of family and friends of those who are better off, the program hopes to bring them together to share their knowledge, their expectations, even their small anxieties. But the women sitting so near to one another seem alone, and many are not bold enough to take from the plates of fruit put out for them.

I approach a young black woman sitting at a table waiting for her name to be called. In spite of the basement surroundings she is dressed as formally as if she were going out on the town, her nails freshly painted and her make up done. She tells me that her name is Deanna and that she is eighteen. "My parents live in London," she says. "That's where I came from. We don't get along very well and that's why I came here two years ago. This is my second— only I had an abortion the first time, so I guess this is my first."

Deanna clearly feels uncomfortable talking and would rather be left alone. Next to her Michelle is sitting and staring ahead. This is Michelle's first visit and she looks glum, half as if she's going to cry and half as if she's going to get mad and storm out of the place. The rings of mascara around her eyes accentuate her bloodless skin and her thin hair has been rinsed blond. Michelle and her boyfriend, she tells me, came here from Vancouver looking for work and live in a bachelor apartment on Carlton Street. Michelle has a job in a print shop but the nurse has told her to give it up. She is certain the baby will be a girl. Would she like to meet some of the other women here? "Sure I would," she says morosely. "I've been in Toronto two years and I haven't made a single friend yet."

But Michelle just sits unmoving until her name is called, picks up the shopping bags, and leaves. The visit seems to have been dispiriting for her rather than otherwise, but perhaps she is the sort of person who would have trouble making friends under any circumstances. One can't blame the system for everything, and it is an insult to these women to think of them as representatives of a class and not as individuals. Nevertheless, it's hard not to believe that Michelle's baby will have a hard time catching up to children whose parents have the leisure time and the resources to shower them with attention, enroll them in music lessons and summer camp, and surround them with the security that makes them believe the world is theirs.

At least Healthy Beginnings will give Michelle a rosier baby. But it is the only program of its kind in Toronto and the number of mothers it helps is small. And even this program has its problems. "I don't like them very much here," says Donna, who is twenty-six and four months pregnant with her second child. Donna, who was born in Guyana, has a wide face and a sardonic smile. She complains of Stop 103, the regular food bank where she tried to come before getting pregnant again but that serves only single people. "Why wouldn't they let me come? Just because I have a kid? And they don't let you take the food you want. Once they had strawberries in little boxes and I asked for a second box. Alberto said no, I'm allowed only one. And later you see them throwing fruit out because it has gone bad. And they make you wait around too long. Why can't they just give me my food and let me go?"

Donna is obviously a self-assured and independent woman without any of Michelle's sense of defeat. Slouched in her chair and sliding her eyes to the side, she even seems to have a deliberately flirtatious air about her. She tells me that she and her five-year-old son live on family benefits of $890 a month but that their basement apartment at Lansdowne and Bloor costs $600. In the past she has been able to make extra money under the table as a waitress but now she's just too big. She still takes her son all the way down to a daycare on Front Street and then picks him up again. "I wouldn't put him in a daycare in our area. I don't like it, there are too many drugs. I can't even let him play with the kids in the neighbourhood. If I do he comes back swearing."

Donna looks not the slightest bit interested in making friends. "I'm not interested in talking to anyone here," she says. "I don't like women. They gossip too much. I never got along with them. I've always preferred the company of men." And looking at me she bestows a Mona Lisa smile.

Among the warren den of basement offices adjacent to the main room is Rick Myer's cluttered desk and above the desk a card has been posted:

REMEMBER THE GOLDEN RULE
Whoever has the gold
Makes the rules

Rick is a sandy-haired man with a lean and lined face that shows his passion for running and bike-riding. It doesn't show that the director of Stop 103 is a minister in the Disciples of Christ Church, a largely American denomination (Rick is from Washington D.C.) with a small Canadian following. "I was preaching social justice for ten years and finally I converted myself," he says. Stop 103 was founded some fifteen years ago, but the demand has grown to 2,000 users a month while its allocation from the central Daily Bread Food Bank has shrunk. This "shortage" (for there is no actual shortage of food in the city) is in spite of the fact that most people use a food bank only when some emergency such as a dental bill causes a deficiency of cash. The people who come to the Stop are refugees (who, Rick says, have the most hopeful expectations of their future), people on social assistance, working people, and some who are homeless. Just last month the Stop had to spend $22,000 on food, and Rick doesn't know where that kind of money is going to keep coming from. Already it allows only single people to come once a month, and now the Stop is considering limiting the area it serves just to keep the numbers manageable. And as Rick notes, the couple of bags of groceries each person can take away once a month really isn't very much.

Like many others, Rick blames the housing crisis for the city's rising poverty. He recognizes the contradiction of his own life, for he and his wife have managed to buy a house, sell it at a profit, and purchase a condominium. "We're the ones who caused it," he shrugs, the lines deepening round his mouth, but he makes a distinction between those who buy a house to live in and mere speculators who drive up prices. He is even sceptical of the provincial money being spent on affordable housing when only twenty-five percent of it actually gets spent on "bricks and mortar" while the rest goes for consultants' salaries, administration and other expenses.

I mention to Rick what seems to me a new and rather glaring social hypocrisy. For months the press and politicians decried the overheated housing market that priced most houses out of the range of even two-income families. Then when prices appeared to drop, that same press, spurred on by real estate agents, panicked over a possible plunge in the market. "I think it's wonderful," Rick nods. "I hope the bottom drops out."

Rick tells how Stop 103 is attempting the difficult move away from the old notion of paternalism in charity— of bestowing favour upon a grateful poor. As an example, he points to the cartons of fruit and vegetables that have been donated from a market on the Danforth, food that has gone too far off for customers to buy. "We have to go picking our way through the stuff to see what we can salvage. But it's demeaning to have to take the food that nobody else wants. I think there's a change for the better in our work, a reinterpretation of how we treat poverty and care about people that is less paternalistic and more a partnership with poor people." I recount to Rick the Roomers meeting where the community workers and the members disagreed on how to solve their food bank problem. "It's kind of scary to us," he says of workers accepting what people want. "But if it is, so be it."

I get up so that Rick can return to work on the Stop's fundraising mailer. Rarely will he give out the names of contributors even to other worthy groups. Dollars are scarce, especially from corporations who prefer to back major sports and arts events that repay the "investment" in good corporate recognition. "Some of them are players in the economic problems," Rick notes, but he's willing to take their money when he can get it.

Rick suddenly tells me that his favourite writers are A.J. Cronin and John Steinbeck. I tell him that Steinbeck is considered sentimental by the critics these days, but he dismisses them with a wave, saying that nobody has written better about the poor. And then to my surprise he says that just a few months ago he became a Canadian citizen and that he felt very proud.

Back in the main room more women have arrived, others have left, and the nurse is moving cheerfully from one to another. At a long table a woman is reading a page with the heading "Breastmilk Production". Her name is Sandra and she is expecting in nine days, she says, which is none too soon. Though the room is cool, Sandra keeps wiping her damp brow. She is unusually tall, with almost red hair, freckled skin, and a firm jaw. She wears a tank top that has the words land of Paradise written on it and that exposes the sides of her flesh-coloured bra. Despite her difficulties, she has a sense of humour that makes her raise her chin and laugh ironically.

Her pregnancy, she says, has been rough. She hasn't felt well and her weight has gone continually up and down. She has little desire to eat, so Betty, the nurse, is trying to get her to drink whipping cream, and although even the thought makes her ill, Sandra is grateful for the advice. "You hear so many things about being pregnant," she says. "Some people tell you old wives' tales. You know, bullshit, whatever you want to call it. They told me that gas pain means you're going to have a hairy baby. If that's true then I'm going to have an ape! But Betty tells me the pains are from the sphincter muscle in the stomach opening from the pressure from the baby. Tums and Rolaids are bad for you— they pass the placenta. She told me to eat cheese."

Not long ago Sandra took her three-year-old, Fernando, and left her husband. Because of her tone, I ask if her husband abused her. "I'd rather not talk about that." The pregnancy was an accident, and pointing to my notepad she says, "Tell everyone that spermicide doesn't work! I can't use the diaphragm or the pill. They say that spermicide is eighty-five percent effective. I have to sit back and laugh. Why did I have to be one of the fifteen in a hundred? I thought about not having it, but my husband said, 'You can't kill my baby.' I guess it was a case of him thinking the baby will solve everything. But I knew it wouldn't and finally, when he was out one day, I took Fernando and our clothes and left. I thought, I can't have anything? Fine, I'll leave anyway. I guess I have a stubborn streak in me. I do get lonely sometimes. Some people say, it's better to have a broken-down car than no car at all. But I'm better off."

Sandra and Fernando fled to a shelter called Robertson House. "It's supposed to be one of the worst in the city. Some of the people are totally wacko, because they're the one shelter that's not allowed to turn anybody away. At times the head staff members had a really pompous attitude. One of them actually said to us, 'Nobody does anything around here unless I say so. And if you don't like it you can leave.' But how can you leave when you have no place to go and welfare won't give you money while you're in the hostel? I guess it's like prison guards. They get onto a power trip."

Sandra is on social assistance for the first time in her life and living in a co-op on Davenport. "I thought I knew how to operate on a tight budget, but that was nothing compared to this. Oh, it gives you a bad attitude towards men," and she laughs but with a serious shake of her head. "It takes two people to make a child, so why is it only one's responsibility? It's a hell of a raw deal. Oh well, I guess it's the feminist in me speaking." This time her laugh means that she has said something daring.

Back in her Winnipeg high school, Sandra was an A student and she hopes that after the baby arrives she can go back to school for computers and accountancy. Right now she's worried about who will take care of Fernando while she's in the hospital. "The doctors are really good," she says of the staff of Women's College Hospital. "They have to put up with my dark and dreary moods, when I say, 'Why am I having this baby?'" Her name is called and she eases out of the chair. "Right now I just want it to be over."

BIRTH ANNOUNCEMENT in the *Globe and Mail:*

JONES/MATHESON— Elizabeth and John are pleased to announce their new issue of preferred stock, Robert Harlan Godfrey on August 5, at the Toronto Hospital. Proud promoters are Mary and Jack Jones, and Louise Matheson. Special thanks to shareholders for their support and happy wishes.

IN THE SALVATION ARMY store on Parliament Street, three women are patiently searching through the bins of clothes or shunting the hangers along the racks. A lanky man whose hair is so blond it's almost white pushes his three-year old daughter in a stroller. She is clutching a stuffed unicorn, worn and a little dirty but nevertheless huggable, and the man pays two dollars at the counter. "Spoil them while you can," he says to the woman behind the register. "I guess I'm just a softy."

"Better than those people who hurt their kids," she answers. "You hear on the news about that woman who burned her baby?"

"Yeah, I'd like to give her what she gives out," he says. "I'd like to string her up and pull out her fingernails."

IN MERRYLAND TOYS on Bloor Street, the nice young fellow with the flat-top hair shows me the selection of Steiff. The stuffed animals from Germany are exquisitely made, coats gorgeously silken and eyes glass-bright. They look remarkably real— almost more than real, as if they were wild animals made tame by magic. Do people really come in and spend so much money for their children?

"The truth is, lots of them buy the animals for themselves," says the fellow with the flat-top. "Some of them have hundreds, they're collectors. Men like the more masculine animals, like these foxes for two hundred and fifty dollars. It's funny how crazy women are about the bears. These here cost four hundred and fifty. Some of them have whole rooms devoted to these things. They come in knowing what animal they want and when they see the price they don't bat an eye."

"You know," he muses, "many people have a misconception that when you work in a toy store like this one you deal with kids all the time. Not so. Kids don't shell out five hundred dollars for a pig."

In a shopping mood, I decide to find out what is selling on Yorkville Avenue. I can remember as a child driving slowly in the car, staring out the back window at the hippies with their long hair, paisley vests and dirty jeans with peace symbols drawn on the knees, sitting on the steps of the Riverboat coffee house. Now I climb the steps of Donato Uomo, an elegantly spare men's store with a polished granite floor that was shipped, Tony Policelli tells me, from Milan. Tony is a young square-jawed man whose oiled hair is brushed precisely into a wave. "We're moving to a more classic, forties look," he says with the slightly clipped consonants characteristic of first generation

Italians. "Double-breasted, but four buttons rather than six. Customers are more sophisticated than when we started. Everyone knows the names of the Italian designers now. Every year there's a price barrier that gets broken— last year it was fifteen hundred dollars. Once they get used to it, people are willing to buy."

In Jeffrey Wald Fine European Jewellery, Lori Wald confirms my sense that Torontonians are learning how to show off their money and position. "They want gaudy!" she almost shouts happily, dropping cigarette ash on the glass cases. Does she ever try to get customers to tone down their taste? "No, because I like gaudy, too." Looking at Lori Wald proves her no liar: a tangle of gold chains hangs round her neck and on her fingers are tremendous studded rings. A punch from a hand wearing one of those rings would leave a waffle pattern on your chin.

"Big, that's the trend," she nods. "Everything big. And more men are coming in and buying themselves jewellery. Two thousand dollars isn't outrageous for a ring. Yorkville is good to us. We do very well here."

Sunshine is pouring over Yorkville Avenue. On the steps of the jewellery store sits a man whose suit jacket is filthy and whose loafers are split at the seams. Compulsively he rubs his hands over his face, up and down, up and down, while women in red heels steer around him and smile to one another, perhaps in embarrassment. The man goes on rubbing, as if to rub himself into invisibility, or perhaps like the bottle of a genie, hoping that something miraculous will emerge, something without pain.

CAROL CONLIN has thoughtfully brewed me a cup of coffee, the bag of beans from the Second Cup on the counter, and we sit on stools in the breakfast nook of her Balmoral Avenue house and chat. Skirts and jackets from Paris hang in a doorway, while the next room is filled with 'fun' jewellery, clocks, and blown glass. Carol shops for the wealthy. She is a tall, tight-skinned woman with a rather severe haircut, her blond-black hair cut short at the sides and spikey at the top, and a lot of lavender eyeshadow under her eyes.

Sitting at the counter I feel uncomfortable, having realized that Carol, who seems a touch nervous, hopes this interview will bring her more business. "My first customer was a client of my husband who is a stock broker," she says, and explains how because people know one another in certain Toronto circles she now gets mostly referrals. Less than two years ago she gave up her job as a court reporter to start Toronto Know-How from an idea that came, naturally, from the United States. Successful men and women in Toronto either don't have time to shop for themselves or are unsure of their own taste. Carol, by shopping for them, takes away the worry. Her clients are accountants, lawyers, advertising executives; she interviews them extensively and examines their wardrobes. Carol takes men to the tailor, helps them choose fabrics and styles, and then selects their shirts and ties.

Carol says, "Last year I called up a man who is a client of mine and said, Colin, don't worry about Brenda's Christmas gift. I've got the perfect thing. And I also found Brenda's gift to Colin, which was an eelskin golfbag the colour of burgundy to match his hair and his car."

I suggest that buying gifts for people is a rather cold prospect. "I see what you mean," she thinks aloud. "It could be cold, but not with the people I have. The women are very grateful that I'm helping their husbands. That way they'll get something they like." Recently she helped a man choose a six thousand dollar mink coat for his wife. "I knew she wanted one and so it was just a matter of timing."

"Most of my male clients are married and their wives are really happy about me. Men here don't pay much attention to their casual clothes and they're usually in bad shape, so we have to work on that. I have a couple of clients who are very flamboyant and they're a lot of fun. In fact, I set one of them up with my very first client— we all had dinner together— and now they're getting married. She's a much more conservative dresser. So I'm beginning to think more in terms of couples dressing together now. She should move more towards his style— and she's in agreement on that. I'm also helping with the wedding, choosing the wedding band and her dress.

"A lot of my women clients are good dressers anyway," she says. "I just help them make it perfect, especially with accessories like earrings and belts. They'll buy a thousand dollar dress and then not know what they should do with it. One woman client of mine is someone without a lot of fashion sense. She had to go to a business cocktail party and she treated it as an evening affair. She found when she got there that she had dressed all wrong. I have to write everything down for her— what goes with what. Right now we're getting ready for her fall wardrobe. She tells me she wants to spend five to eight thousand dollars. We know so far that we're getting one leather outfit. She has so much more confidence now. It's true that when you look good you feel good."

The telephone rings. "If we can get the material by Thursday..." she tells a client. At a ten percent commission, Carol herself is not growing rich, but she enjoys making aesthetic choices for people far more than sitting in a courtroom all day. When she's off the phone I ask whether she thinks her clients are spoiled.

Carol concentrates so as to answer truthfully. "Some of them are, of course, but some of them are not. They're just working really hard."

FOR DINNER at the Christian Resource Centre it's "Newfie steak," as Michael Shapcott calls it— thick slices of balogna, along with white buns, chopped iceberg lettuce, and potato salad. Tonight's meeting is the Basic Poverty Action Group, whose members are community workers and low-income people and we line up around the make-shift buffet table with our plates. Of the many reform and anti-poverty groups in Toronto, I have decided to frequent those working out of the CRC. Because of their location in Regent Park, the diversity of their membership, and their philosophy of "community development" rather than charity, these groups will, I hope, lead me to a fuller understanding of both poverty and activism. And also I feel challenged by Michael Shapcott's scepticism of my project, for he himself is a former journalist who believes that understanding comes not from observation, but only from involvement.

Involved or not, I honestly don't know how they can keep eating this stuff at their meetings; just smelling it makes me lose my appetite. The potato salad tastes vile and while taking a few desultory bites I think of the conversation just this morning with Franco Prevedello, owner of the restaurant Centro. Every night Centro's tables are fully booked and patrons squeeze past the Italianate columns and oxblood-leather chairs to pat shoulders and compare wines. I asked

Franco whether he agreed with the character in the movie *When Harry Met Sally* who calls dining out the theatre of the eighties. "Absolutely," said Franco. Some of his customers come every night; they treat his restaurant like an extension of their own dining rooms.

The food in the basement of the Regent Park church might not include peppered beef carpaccio or a special from the mesquite grill, but the people settling around the table are open and friendly and nobody questions my being here or acts suspicious in the presence of a notebook. Instead, they seem glad just to have another interested person around. Parika, who appears to attend the meetings of all the CRC's groups, comes over to say hello. As the meeting starts I sit beside a man with a young face but long greying hair pulled back into a ponytail. He speaks clearly and precisely, conveying information, leading the discussion towards decisions with speed, for he has two more meetings to attend tonight. Watching him, I slowly come to feel that his face is familiar. "David?" I say, and turning, he recognizes me. He is David Kidd, who was a younger-looking community worker running the Cabbagetown Community Arts Centre during my brief stint as a local newspaper editor six or seven years ago. All these years that I've been away from the neighbourhood David has remained, organizing low-income people, lobbying city hall, plugging away. This amazes me— I already feel lethargic from the few hours of talk, the disagreements on strategy, the effort that must go into even small acts of opposition.

As the meeting moves from one agenda topic to another, this very subject of fatigue keeps rearing its head. There are simply not enough people to do all the work; those who are involved are over-extended. A question comes up of merging the Basic group with the organization called March against Poverty. Michael Shapcott had hoped that the March would organize around underdeveloped issues such as poverty and women, building community bridges that would increase the power of the anti-poverty groups. But as that hasn't happened there's no point in duplicating efforts. Meanwhile, someone at the table notes that most of the members of Basic are white community workers of almost the same age. Other kinds of people just aren't being reached.

Carmel Hili, the CRC worker who is a former Jesuit priest, wants to organize a popular culture festival across from the proposed site of the ballet opera house at Bay and Wellesley. The province's housing first policy is supposed to mean that surplus provincial land be used to build affordable housing, but the province has promised the valuable downtown site and sixty-five million dollars if the federal government will kick in another seventy million and the metro government twenty. The opera house is one of the city's "megaprojects"— along with the bids for the 1996 Olympics and the world's fair in the year 2000— that are being opposed by yet another CRC group called the Bread Not Circuses Coalition. The popular culture festival, Carmel says, would show that the anti-poverty groups aren't against culture, just elite culture that only the wealthy can afford.

But Tammie Mayes, the young CRC worker, says that she's having trouble getting volunteers to run No Place Like Home, an annual event meant to organize the homeless and publicize the need for affordable housing. Several of the workers from St. Christopher House agree. They've got a drop-in centre to run five days and three nights a week and are already short-staffed. The voices around the table sound guarded and weary. But just before a vote to cancel the festival is taken, Michael Shapcott speaks. "Let's not talk about what we can't do," he says with energy. "Let's talk about what we can do." He reminds everyone that Basic has been active on the opera house issue for two years, that it is only being asked to support the festival, and that people always come through at the last minute. Like a good general, he rallies the troops before the charge; enthusiasm sparks around the table. The resolution to support the festival passes.

But there are more issues to discuss and everyone sounds tired. As the meeting winds down, one of the women from St. Christopher house jumps up and screams. We all watch a fat cockroach wade nonchalantly across the floor.

After the meeting, Parika waits for me, and together we walk across Dundas. She has taken on the role of debriefer over a coffee at the one table by the take-out counter of George's Spaghetti House. Tonight she is wearing her "official outfit"— the pullover, grey blazer and pleated skirt. Parika dresses more neatly than many people in the neighbourhood, a sign of her sense of personal dignity.

On our way to George's we run into Judy, a friend of Parika's from the time they were both homeless and sleeping in hostels, and Parika asks her to join us. Judy looks to be in her forties, and her manner is rather girlish. As we sit in George's she tells us how family difficulties and ill health ended her secretarial career, but just as in listening to Parika sometimes, I can't quite put the pieces together. "What happened to your tooth?" Parika asks. Which tooth Parika is referring to is hard to tell, for Judy has three or four that are dark or broken. "Calcium deficiency," Judy shrugs.

Parika and Judy talk about living in hostels. "It's not the hostel itself," Judy says. "Every one of them seems to have a person working there who shouldn't be dealing with people." Parika tells how the hostels throw out your belongings after forty-eight hours but don't warn you beforehand. A person can stay in the same hostel for two weeks before having to move. "There is no sense to this rotation," she says. Tired of dragging her possessions around, Parika discarded them one by one, until she was left with nothing but the dirty clothes on her back.

Judy gets up to go. Her heart problem is improving, she says, and she hopes to begin office work again. She also mentions her interest in cartooning, writing, and various other projects and it's impossible to assess whether she's being realistic.

"I'm getting tired of these meetings," Parika sighs after Judy has gone. "I don't know about you, but all this talk is exhausting me. And the food they serve! Did you eat the potato salad? It is terrible. You know, when I shop I don't do it in the east end even though I live here. I go to Parkdale or somewhere else. I don't like to stay around here, it's depressing. There are so many poor people. Have you seen the neighbourhoods in Willowdale?" she asks, unknowingly naming the suburb where I grew up. "Nice houses, nice trees. That's where I would like to live."

Parika tells how she enrolled in part-time high school after her job training course. But she had too much difficulty concentrating and plans to start again in the fall with the hope of getting a high school diploma. She will take science courses, anything that doesn't require writing. That surprises me as Parika, despite her tendency to change subjects with dizzying rapidity, is highly articulate. It is she who should write her story down, not filtered through my limitations and assumptions, but told by her own voice, with her acerbic yet generous opinions intact. As I tell her this I remember some lines by the poet Erin Mouré—

> Several parts of this poem are encoded to prevent theft
> of language

and wonder if Parika's own language is in some obscure way just so encoded. Perhaps that is why I can't always understand her; perhaps trying to write down her words is a kind of theft of her voice and her power.

But Parika smiles and shakes her head. "Once I took English, and the teacher told us to describe a flower. I wrote, *The flower is beautiful.* She said that was no good, that "beautiful" wasn't descriptive. I had to write what colour it was and so on. But I couldn't do any more than that."

Parika changes the subject: she wants to talk about family violence, male aggression, and Philippe Rushton's theories of racial difference. And then suddenly she speaks of her family who, despite their living in Toronto, she doesn't see anymore.

"I don't think about them very much," she says. "But you know, it's funny. Sometimes at night I dream about them."

On the street, Parika and I say goodbye. I walk west on Dundas Street, dark but for the streetlights overhead and the lights in the shop and restaurant windows. Just over a hundred years ago Toronto got its first electric arc lamps. At Pembroke Street five prostitutes are standing, an unusually large number. Further on is the Filmore Hotel, where I once attended a stag party. One of the groom's friends, a just-graduated law student who had drunk too much, sat in a chair, and, while a naked woman table danced before him, howled, *I'm a Bay Street lawyer! I'm a Bay Street lawyer!* Now, two men dressed in Italian loafers and dress pants come out the Filmore's doors. As they walk beside me one is finishing a story—

"I was in one booth and my partner in the deal was in the other booth."

"Yeah?"

"And we both got sucked off."

"How was it?"

"Oh, it was okay."

"Even the worst is fantastic, eh?"

"Right! There was this other woman, I used to visit her once in a while. This one New Year's Eve we did it right in the back of a cab, at the stroke of midnight. Now she wants to go into catering."

"No kidding. My wife knows everybody in the catering business... "

I walk on faster in order to get away and pause at Victoria Street, beside the Ryerson sculpture, a lifeless series of rising blocks spiralling around a large bronze bird. After a moment I realize that a man is staring at me from a few feet away. He's grizzled looking, obviously drunk, and holding a steel pipe in his hand. Without taking his eyes from me he drops the pipe and its clattering makes me jump. The man picks up the pipe again and mutters, "Judas... Jews... " Then he swings the pipe hard against the granite block, near my head. "Watch out," I say, taking a step back, and, sensing my fear, he takes a step towards me. But he turns away and walks into the crowd moving towards Yonge Street. Standing there, I can hear at periodic intervals the clanging of the pipe.

AT MIDNIGHT, I crouch beside the toilet, waiting for another wave of nausea. Closing my eyes as it comes, I remember. The potato salad.

Cheap Entertainment

FORUMS, MEETINGS, conferences. So many forums on the crises in the city— on minorities and the police, development, the needs of women— forums with such a disparate range of conflicting solutions that I think of Chekhov's *The Cherry Orchard* and a remark of the character, Gayev: *If a lot of cures are suggested for a disease, it means that the disease is incurable.*

But there is a more positive way of thinking about these public events; as opportunities for people to hear and to speak. Attending them, I am amazed by how strangely real such events feel, and how the expression of outrage and impotence from people as their city becomes more unlivable makes my own pulse race in sympathy. The next day, when I read the press coverage or watch it on television, I am dully surprised not only by how reductive is the reporting, but how distant the event feels, as if it took place in another city or even another time. As if it had nothing to do with me.

The forum on Toronto's economy was one of a series held at the St. Lawrence Centre and it was there that people could hear in words what was visible in the streets, the growing disparity of wealth in the city. Linda Torney, president of the Labour Council of Metropolitan Toronto, told how the lost industrial jobs are getting replaced by low-paying service-sector jobs. Peter Tomlinson, the city government's director of economic development, spoke in jargonese: "It's the best of times in terms of macro-economic numbers and the worst in terms of micro-economic restructuring going on that is directly following from the boom conditions at the macro-economic level." In other words, at the same time that Toronto is experiencing a building explosion and the lowest unemployment since wartime, a lot of people in the city are actually losing ground. Linda Torney called it a "tale of two cities"— of the rich getting richer and the poor getting poorer.

After the forum I visited Peter Tomlinson in his city hall office. He said that service-sector jobs now make up over fifty percent of the jobs in the city, a reverse from the Toronto of the 1950s when manufacturing jobs were most numerous. Those manufacturing jobs are disappearing for the most part because of rising land values: the plants are sitting on property so valuable that companies can sell out and move from the city, profiting by millions of dollars. The problem for Toronto, Tomlinson said, is that the economy loses the diversity that makes it resistant to recession. And although all the evidence isn't in yet, Tomlinson himself believes that those blue-collar jobs are being replaced by lower-paying service-sector work— what are becoming known sardonically as "McJobs." But I asked him what the city could really do. He'd already noted at the forum that provincial law often prevents city governments from interfering in industrial land deals, and even if it could I wondered how effective was meddling in the free market economy. "No one's denying it might be more efficient just to let the market forces work," Tomlinson said, but he asked aloud what this loss of diversity will do to the city.

For another public meeting I walked east on Shuter Street to Park Public School, a wonderfully immense building of red stone with an entrance flanked by tremendous columns. Upstairs in the teachers' lounge Reform Toronto was having its first public meeting. The group was formed the year before at Gennaro's Tavern by a handful of people unhappy about the direction the city was taking and especially about the land deals made between developers and politicians. Reform Toronto wanted to affect the election by informing people how the city and metropolitan councils work and just how the councillors have been voting. Its members worked hard during the election to back the reform candidates, and could take some credit for getting many of them elected, ousting from their seats the "old guard" who had comfortably held their positions for years.

Judging by the crowd, Reform Toronto and its supporters are quite different from the groups at the Christian Resource Centre. The people here were university educated, downtown dwellers by choice, professionals. This group too favoured affordable housing, but rather than concentrating on one issue, it backed a whole slate, from cleaning up the Don River to making the arts more accessible to people. Chris Green, editor of *The Badger*, the group's newspaper, told the audience that anyone who wanted to could work on the publication. "In Toronto," he said, "there's a real tendency just to buy the newspaper and see what the media says." Instead, Reform Toronto's paper is put out by people in an open, democratic, collective manner.

But Chris Green sparked angry words from some people and for a moment it appeared as if the meeting might dissolve in dissension and anger. "There's some reforming of Reform Toronto that has to be done," said a man with swept-back grey hair. Apparently, the submissions by the group's various committees for the latest edition of *The Badger* had been completely re-written by the editors and some of the people on the committees were mad. I felt as if I were reading some history of the left, in which the people interested in reform destroy themselves without any help from the opposition.

ALTHOUGH I first met Parika at the Cathedral Square meeting, I had actually seen her earlier at the special hearing of the Toronto Board of Health. The hearing, on the subject of "poverty and health," was held in the comfortable hand-me-down lounge of St. Christopher House on Queen Street and it was there that Parika spoke eloquently of the inadequacy of hostels, which don't care about health, Parika said, but only that homeless people shouldn't die on the streets and get written about in the press.

The hearing was crowded with health professionals, reporters, and a few activists and people of low income; but like almost all such meetings there were few if any present who did not have some direct stake in health care; few were citizens simply concerned with the welfare of their city. Nevertheless, the goals of the board of health, at least on paper, seem marvelously enlightened. It has commissioned and accepted a report called Healthy City 2000 which recognizes that inequalities in the health care system result in poor people having shorter, more illness-ridden lives. The attainment of good health, the report states, requires more than just access to doctors and drugs, but to good nutrition, education, work, and housing.

During that meeting the board heard about rising demands on food banks, about literacy programs, and how depression among the unemployed and de-institutionalized leads to illness. Of course, not everyone speaks well at such meetings and already I was getting accustomed to hearing people drone on repetitively or make strange and touching spectacles of themselves. One woman of Asian descent, whose purported reason for speaking was to report on an anti-smoking program, talked about her family's successful assimilation into the city's life and broke out into hysterical weeping. Another man, on hearing a report on suicide and family breakdown among injured workers, stood up to speak. "My brother lost his left hand and instead of a pension was given a lump sum," the man said. "He was so depressed by this that he left the country and went to Mexico."

But one woman mesmerized both the audience and the board. Her name was Pat Capponi. She wore a large black hat with a red feather in it, and she spoke quietly but insistently, taking the occasional drag on her cigarette as she told how ex-psychiatric patients like herself were stereotyped and ghettoized. "Our people don't go to the professionals because they tend to get their kids snatched," she said offhandedly. Even when governments asked for their views, they always had to sit on the other side of the table, as advisors rather than decision-makers. She told how the removal of stomach bitters from the shelves of variety stores meant that more people were now sniffing glue. The decision makers don't know what their impact is on a group "whose only pleasures are cigarettes and coffee."

A member of the Board of Health asked her if she might write a special report for the board, but Pat Capponi declined. So few people from her community were willing or capable of speaking up that her services were already too much in demand. In fact, she was at the meeting for a positive reason, as one of the founders of the Gerstein Centre, a new temporary home for ex-psychiatric patients that had taken years of effort to organize and fund.

While I listened, a middle-aged man came up to speak to me. He introduced himself as Stan Josey, a reporter for the *Star*; having noticed my notebook, he good-naturedly assumed that I was part of the same flock. But as we talked I thought, no, I'm not like you, or at least I don't want to be. It's the woman talking about homelessness whose side I want to be on, not the side of the professional press. But perhaps I was fooling myself, I realized, perhaps being an observer rather than someone living with homelessness or illiteracy or the stigma of having been a psychiatric patient— perhaps being someone with a notepad put me on one side whether I liked it or not.

WALKING ACROSS Nathan Phillips Square, I pause by the tiny peace garden that was put here in 1984, a place of stillness in the hectic downtown. There is something quietly sad about the unfinished roof overhead and the pool beneath, into which water from Hiroshima was once poured. Standing here is a good place to contemplate the proposed twinning of Toronto with the Soviet city of Volgograd. City council defeated the motion after pressure from emigré groups from the Soviet bloc. That seems a misunderstanding of a token gesture of friendship and that we aren't twins with the people of Volgograd seems to deepen the garden's sadness.

Emerging from the garden, I am addressed by a tall black man, neatly greying at the temples and wearing a worn three-piece suit. As he asks for change his voice is deep and refined: "I've been suffering a good deal lately." On the stage set up at the side of the square a line of Ukrainian folk dancers is kicking away to the sound of recorded music.

Today is special, for I have never been in council chambers before. Like most people, I have never influenced or even watched the council meetings where votes are taken. Today's is not a regular council meeting, but the opening of Cityplan 91, a four-day conference to launch the writing of Toronto's new land-use plan that will go into effect in 1991. The plan, which sets the guidelines for how the city progresses, which allows or forbids residential, commercial, and industrial development, is the city's strongest tool for shaping its own future. City council and its planners, aware that Toronto is at a crossroads, is bringing in experts from England, the Netherlands, the United States, and across Canada— planners, urban economists, transportation specialists, ecologists, directors of housing and health— to provide the council with experience and advice.

Part of the concept of Cityplan 91 is to allow people in the city to be active participants in the writing of the plan, to make the plan responsible to the citizens. But that goal is off to a shaky start, for the curving council chamber is less than half full, and many of those present are city planners, developers, and other interested parties. The council has failed miserably in publicizing the event.

Perhaps the council shouldn't only be blamed, but the people too for not coming out— that's my thought as I spot the regular faces that are visible at so many of these public meetings. Making my way down to the first row, I sit down beside a woman named Lynn. I'd first met Lynn a couple of weeks before, at the annual meeting of Neighbourhood Information Post, beside the Parliament Street Library. We had sat together then, listening to the report of the Post's health program, while Lynn ate from a plate of fruit from the buffet. As the social workers reported on their programs, Lynn leaned over and said, "Oh, they're well-meaning people. But sometimes they say condescending things without meaning to. I prefer to look after myself. You know what the best way to find out information is? Don't come to a place like this, ask another poor person. I have a friend, an old alcoholic, he's told me how to deal with the system. Poor people don't like to be helped all the time because it's a humiliating experience. That's why so many don't come to places like this."

While we were talking, one of the Post's staff members, a well-groomed elderly woman wearing a black skirt and pearls, came up to chat with Lynn. "Tomorrow I'm going off on holiday," the woman said. "I haven't had one since last March."

"I worked at one job, for a social agency," Lynn said. "Every week I put in sixteen hours overtime and never got paid."

"Really," smiled the woman. And went off to speak to another staff member.

Now Lynn and I wait for the Cityplan forum to begin. "I go to a lot of political meetings," she says. "Because they're free. That's my main source of entertainment. I think this is just a token to give the appearance of citizen involvement. Look at the speakers— they're all Conservative or Liberal flunkies."

I look down at my program. The speakers for the opening are not the out-of-town experts but local celebrities— Harry Brown, the broadcaster, Jean Augustine, the head of the Metropolitan Toronto Housing Authority who replaced John Sewell after his contract wasn't renewed, Jane Pepino, a development lawyer, Robert Fulford, the journalist, and Eb Zeidler, the architect who designed the Eaton Centre. As the forum begins, Harry Brown tells us that Toronto is responsible for giving the world pablum. Jean Augustine talks about the "scourge of drug dealing." ("She's phoney as a wooden nickel," says Lynn). Robert Fulford, balding and rotund, tells how important the arts are to the city. But he doesn't mention the vibrant small theatres or the young painters searching for affordable studio space— those artists who express the city's character and provoke their audiences with daring work. Fulford mentions only the big, official institutions— the opera, the ballet, the Art Gallery of Ontario— and he spends the rest of his allotted time decrying the fact that Toronto's rich are not collectors and donators of art.

Eb Zeidler, the architect, is a suave and intellectual European who as a young man studied at the Bauhaus. He shows slides of Copenhagen and of Paris and he admiringly calls the cafés of Paris "the living rooms of the people." He uses grand terms such as "the beautiful city" and he expresses a hatred for visual clutter— telephone poles and newspaper boxes.

After the last speaker the audience is invited to ask questions and people come down from their seats to line up dutifully at the microphones. Although this is purportedly a public forum, Harry Brown insists that questions be short and he cuts people off or badgers them not to make statements but only to ask questions.

Pat Capponi, the woman who had so impressed the Board of Health, gets to the microphone. She says, "Though the boulevards of Paris are the living rooms of the people, the streets of Toronto are the bedrooms of the people." She accuses the panel of not truly reflecting the city because its members are all privileged and wealthy.

"Who's privileged?" says Robert Fulford, raising his voice and arching his eyebrows. "Do you think someone gave me *Saturday Night?* I was a poor boy." His belligerence stuns the audience. He seems unaware that the character of poverty has changed since his own day and that a person can no longer work himself up from copyboy.

A man with a European accent at the microphone says, "We must judge a city by how it treats the disenfranchised, not how it treats the rich. I have ideas and I'm sure many others here do too. But I can't convey them in two minutes." Nevertheless, he isn't given more. The members of the panel, however, are given as much time as they like to respond to the questioners. Lynn reaches the microphone and nervously asks Eb Zeidler a question. How can he see the city as an "aesthetic object" when his own creation, the Eaton Centre, is frequented by homeless people who are constantly being thrown out by security staff?

Eb Zeidler answers by asking if the lady at the microphone has seen the film *Babette's Feast.* It doesn't occur to him that some people can't afford to go to movies and without waiting for an answer he begins to praise the film's protagonist, a woman chef who spends all her money on a single extraordinary meal, giving all that she has to her art although the expense will leave her with nothing. The holding up for example of this sacrifice for art's sake seems presumptuous from a man whose own work has made him wealthy and famous. And he adds, how wonderful that the same bench in the Eaton Centre can be occupied by a dozing derilect and a woman in a mink coat. He seems deliberately unaware that unlike a public street, a mall is private property, and while the woman in the mink is allowed to linger as long as she likes, the derilect is firmly removed.

The opening of Cityplan 91 has taken on a strange atmosphere, as if some static disconnection is interfering with the communication between the floor and the rising tiers of seats. From the audience comes a feeling of hostility and anger, from the panelists defensiveness and camaraderie. A question is asked by a young man who calls himself a photographer and at last the panel can show its whole-hearted enthusiasm. The young man calls for the formation of an "art-deco society" to fight for the preservation of the city's historic buildings. Robert Fulford considers the young man an ideal citizen and the other panelists nod in agreement. And this adoring praise makes me suddenly angry. Because I too love the city's finest buildings— the Victorian warehouses of Front Street, the Great Hall of Union Station, the Romanesque houses of the Annex— and believe that such architecture should be preserved. But a city is a living place, not a museum, and it makes me angry that I am forced to choose sides— the present over the past, the living over the dead.

Lynn, having asked her question, has sat down again in the audience. She stares forward through her glasses, her hands in her lap.

Schmoozing

SLIDING INTO Toronto at midnight in a borrowed Pontiac, along the QEW to the Gardiner, when the city suddenly appears against the black reflecting surface of the lake and the curve of the harbour. And the city dark, but strewn with hundreds— thousands— of lights, rising up the towers, tossed across the cityscape.

Swiftly the car passes the illuminated Palais Royale where Benny Goodman and Duke Ellington used to swing. During the war, when Count Basie and his all-black band played the Palais, Toronto blacks had to stand outside to listen. The car slides up University Avenue, past the darkened fronts of office towers and glowing bars, slowing for a man who crosses the street in imitation of Groucho Marx's cigar-pointing stride, trenchcoat flapping. Then Queen's Park Crescent, the hushed campus of the University of Toronto, and Bloor Street with a burst of city life— record stores and bookshops and the all-night Super Save. Loud men in university jackets spill out of the Brunswick House to be looked upon with condescending amusement by the habitués of the sidewalk café tables. As always, the grizzled young man with the slow speech is hawking tomorrow's *Globe*. At the corner of Albany and Bloor, a woman steps from the curb, gets honked at, and steps back again with a little dance, whirling her red skirt like a fan.

On the streets radiating from Bloor Street West— Madison, Robert, Palmerston, Euclid— the prices and rents keep rising but the mix is still compatible and human— students in their bachelor apartments, artist couples in their flats, downtown professionals in open-concept houses; and, a little west, still the multi-generational families of immigrants. My first apartment was on Madison, with a tiny porch all my own and almost no heat. Later a flat on Shaw Street, where my mother, a teenager in the early forties, had moved with her family up from Nassau Street in Kensington Market. And where my father's family, refugees from Europe, also landed. It was my paternal grandmother who wept when she saw the low, grey, muddy landscape of Toronto. Like Warsaw, a backwards town. Eventually the families did well; they joined the caravan moving up Bathurst Street to the suburbs. But ghosts of their younger selves make this neighbourhood more real to me than anywhere else. More home.

Of course Toronto has changed, and so has Bloor Street West. The café chairs at By-the-Way are rickety and spattered with paint. It is the kind of restaurant where the waiters are chosen for their ennui and someone is always writing a poem inside a paperback copy of *One Hundred Years of Solitude*. Where cappuccinos are drunk while the latest absurdist clown show by Dean Gilmour at the Poor Alex is debated. The kind of restaurant that I am always expecting to grow out of and hope I never do.

And always there is the rush after the film at the Bloor Cinema gets out. The Bloor Cinema is the heart of the neighbourhood, but it has been bought by a developer and its future is uncertain. The Bloor not exist? With a wince I recall the line of Baudelaire: that a city changes, alas, more quickly than a mortal's heart. Once, at the Bloor, a man wandered down the darkened rows of the cinema just as the film was starting, and in a desperate voice called out, "Irene, where are you?" A beat later the audience began to sing:

Goodnight, Irene
Goodnight, Irene
Irene, Goodnight
I'll see you in my dreams

At a table, a young woman in an African cap sips her Corona and says, "Isn't this a wonderful place? In five minutes everybody in the world I know walks by."

TELEPHONING the Cluny Corporation, I reach a secretary in the office of Robert Bandeen. She puts me off, saying that Mr. Bandeen is really too busy a man and that I ought to speak to the publicist for Metropolitan Toronto. I insist that Mr. Bandeen is Metro's newly appointed "special representative" to business around the world, and it is he to whom I wish to speak on the subject of Toronto's booming economy.

"Mr. Bandeen loves to talk about the city," she says, softening. "You promise that you won't be rough on him, nothing nasty, no questions about conflict-of-interest or that sort of thing? Because I sit just outside his door and you'll have to get past me." We laugh. "All right," she says, "I'll go out on a limb for you. I'm very protective of him, you see. I don't want to find any niggers in the woods. Oh, one isn't supposed to use that expression any more. I mean coloured people in the woods."

And I get my appointment, all very jolly.

Hanging up, I recall a couple of other recent conversations. One was at the public forum on Ataratiri, the new neighbourhood to be built on old industrial land east of the St. Lawrence neighbourhood. The forum was held at the Berkeley Street Theatre and in the crowd was Jane Jacobs, the wise and now elderly guru of city planning, whose book, *The Death and Life of Great American Cities*, is still a beacon of common sense about what makes cities safe and livable. Unable to reach Ms. Jacobs during the intermission because of the crowd, I turned instead to a petite woman standing alone, wearing a National Ballet T-Shirt knotted at the bottom. "I live right on Trinity Street, on the edge of the project they're going to build," she said, and told me that she worked for the Toronto Stock Exchange. "I'm concerned. When I bought my condominium a year ago they told me there wouldn't be any high-rise building in the area. And now they're talking about a big development! And I'm also worried about the social mix, the kinds of people that will live there. Toronto's getting too crowded, with all the immigrants coming in. I can't even walk through Chinatown anymore. I'm starting to feel like a minority in my own city."

That same day, as I waited for a bus on Dufferin, a woman asked me how often the buses ran. She was black, conservatively dressed and with a lilting West Indian accent. "Toronto is a very beautiful city," she said as we sat together on the bus. "But the white people haven't yet learned to cope. I'm in the nursing profession. The things patients call me and say to me, demanding this and that! They don't treat you like a human being. There's no friendship there. The white people, they won't do these jobs, they leave them to us.

"When I came to this country I worked cleaning people's houses," she went on. "Big houses, out in Markham and places like that. Those people, they take advantage of you if you don't yet have your Social Insurance Number. And they don't treat you properly. They don't really care for you. It's not the real white people I'm complaining about, the real British I mean. It's the Italians and the Jews. They're the ones with the money and the power. They control the city."

She must have sensed a change in me, for she soon stopped talking.

ROBERT BANDEEN drives his Jaguar from the house in Rosedale to the office on Toronto Street near the King Edward Hotel in just over ten minutes. But then Robert Bandeen has the driving habits of a transplanted Montrealer, a secretary tells me as I wait for him to arrive. Presently chief executive officer of an investment firm called the Cluny Corporation, Mr. Bandeen is the former chairman of Crown Life, former CEO of Canadian National, enjoys more than a dozen other business connections, has been awarded several honorary degrees and the Order of Canada, and is a member of the York and Toronto clubs.

When he sweeps into the office I am surprised at how big a man Robert Bandeen is; he is one of those few whose baldness contributes to virility. As we sit down I ask him about his new position as Metro's special representative to business. "I feel that if you live in a community you should give something back to it," he says. "I've never done anything like this before. And I'm amazed that Toronto isn't better known. A lot of people haven't been here and so in a way I'm doing missionary work."

For his efforts Mr. Bandeen receives one dollar a year. He has just returned from his first trip to England where he attempted to woo the CEOs of foreign corporations with the wonders of relocating their head offices to Toronto. The most likely companies are those undergoing restructuring after mergers, acquisitions, or corporate buy-outs, and Robert Bandeen attacks them with what he calls the "rifle approach." Metro can then wine and dine executives from a two-million dollar a year budget. More corporate headquarters, Mr. Bandeen says, bring employees and salaries, use lawyers and other services of the city, and so benefit the community. What makes Toronto an easy sell is its dominating financial infrastructure: headquarters of the five major banks and most of the investment houses in the country, accountancy and advertising firms, direct flights to the rest of the world. Adding a low crime rate relative to American cities and what Mr. Bandeen calls its growing cultural sophistication and "desire for international excellence" makes for a very attractive package.

Mr. Bandeen does not fear that more head offices in the city will cause land prices to rise even higher and erode what industrial jobs the city has left. "It's the natural change of things," he says. "Looking down the line to the future, it just doesn't make sense to try and bring in industry. If they'd asked me to do that I would have turned them down flat! How can blue-collar workers pay two hundred and fifty thousand dollars for a house? How could we live without foreign investment? Look at the data. The only way we can manage our debt is with the foreign money coming in. Any move to restrict foreign capital has to be paid for in a lower standard of living. Without foreign investment we're going to stagnate. We're part of the whole global market."

Robert Bandeen may be right; certainly it's true that Toronto has been a trading town for over a hundred and fifty years and that without the markets of Britain and then the United States it would never have grown into a major city. But like many businessmen, Robert Bandeen looks at the larger picture and sees that an increase in absolute wealth is always good. In any case, it isn't business that he wants to talk about, but the arts. As a 'senator' of the Stratford Festival, board member of the Art Gallery of Ontario, and chairman of Toronto's first International Choral Festival, he moves in the most glamorous of the city's artistic circles. Speaking of his first stay in Toronto back in 1971, he remembers the city as "Scottish and dour. It used to be almost impossible to get a decent meal in the city. I used to feel desperate trying to find a place to eat after a show at the O'Keefe or the symphony. The Royal York was supposed to be the best. You had to have a strong constitution to eat there often. We came back ten years later and the city was unrecognizable."

Listening to Robert Bandeen, I nod in sympathy. His taste and natural sophistication make him easy to like. Unlike many business people who sit on arts boards for the prestige and contacts, Mr. Bandeen expresses genuine passion, particularly for classical music and opera. He eloquently compares Montreal's symphony (better conductor) to Toronto's ("it has all the horses"). He judges with discrimination the level of Toronto opera-goer's maturity: "Berlioz is not popular in Toronto, nor I think, understood." But even as I listen with pleasure, it occurs to me that Robert Bandeen sees Toronto as something like New York, or something like Paris, or something like Vienna. That he judges it not by any indigenous qualities (it might as well have none) but how close it can come to adopting the dress of other cities.

The artistic contribution to Toronto that Robert Bandeen is most proud of is the International Choral Festival. Conceived with an open vision of cultural diversity, it has brought to the city the Boys Choir of Harlem, the Tibetan Temple Singers, and the Poliansky Choir of Moscow. And unlike the exorbitant prices for so many shows here, shutting out people of low and even moderate income, Robert Bandeen has helped to insure that ticket prices are reasonable. And all over the city, in churches and community halls, concerts are free to everyone. The choirs, not business, are what Robert Bandeen wants to talk about.

"The Bulgarians are stunning," he says admiringly.

AFTER LEAVING Robert Bandeen's office, I walk towards St. James Cathedral. On a grassy plain across from the St. Lawrence Centre, two workmen are setting up a drum set on a stage— one of the sites for the current jazz festival. At their best, such events connect us to the rest of the world. I remember how electric was Salman

Rushdie's reading at the International Festival of Authors the previous year, and how his presence here made the later threat on his life more tangible and cruel, as if he were one of our citizens, too.

The spire of St. James Cathedral is the second highest on the continent, after St. Patrick's in New York. In the coolness I take a place on one of the wooden pews that face the massive pipes of the organ. On the stage are fifty girls and young women, in white blouses with red sashes round the waist, holding their music folders in their hands under the illuminated windows. These are the Amabile Youth Singers, giving one of the choral festival's free concerts, and their high voices fill the vaulted interior with Aaron Copland's "Ching-a-Ring-Char." Some hundred and fifty people sit listening with rapt attention. Although the concert is free the audience is white and, by their dress, decidedly middle-class, and it occurs to me how rarely one sees people of low income at these free events. Why is it that the people who take advantage of them are the same who can pay for their pleasures? The people who are confident of their place in the city.

Agnus Dei, the voices sing in little swelling waves. And then the descending *Amen*, repeated and repeated to a final still note.

ON A SOUTHBOUND train of the University subway sits a man in his early thirties, tall, with a drooping cowboy moustache and wearing a black cowboy hat. In the pinch on each side of the hat is pinned an enamel swastika. Is it really possible to see two neo-Nazis in the subway in the same week? The first was a slim boy with close-cropped hair whose Doc Marten boots made his feet look ridiculously large. Now this man across from me brings on a nauseating fear and anger. Part of me wants to get up and pummel him, tear off that damn hat and stomp it into the floor. But his hands are as big as catchers' mitts and his knuckles bony. Besides, as a law-abiding citizen I understand the destructiveness of violence and how one can become what one hates. So instead I want to get up, point to him, and announce to everyone on the train that we are in the presence of a fascist, a hater of blacks and Jews and gays, a poison in the city. But I just sit, not even looking into his shaded glasses.

PAST THE PEELING green door and up the dim stairs of the small brick building on Wolseley Street is the studio, a high-ceilinged chaos of big canvases leaning on paint-splattered walls and bathed in dusty light, of ancient furniture with the stuffing bursting out, of piles of dusty books and a makeshift kitchen in a corner. And three bleary-eyed artists drinking their first cup of morning coffee.

Andy Fabo, Stephen Andrews, and Michael Balser are sitting around the wooden table talking in blurry voices. Michael is a video maker while Stephen draws on canvas, and Andy, the best known of the three, paints and makes videos with Michael. They are all from other places— Fredericton, Sarnia, Calgary— and came to Toronto not only to be better arists but because they are gay. Stephen, the youngest, and Andy both have works in the Homogenius show at Mercer Union that opened to coincide with Gay Pride Day. It is the most important day in the year for the city's gay community, chosen not to commemorate any Toronto event but for the Stonewall riot in New York. And it is a day that city council once again refused to recognize officially, preferring instead "Harold Ballard Day" and "Purebred Dog Week." That sexuality matters for Stephen and Andy is shown by their work hanging on the Mercer Union's high white walls; Stephen's enigmatic triptych on three large mylar sheets focused on two drawn figures of men engaged in sex, and Andy's almost primitive painting showed two men with erections crossed like swords.

Andy is chubby-faced and wears his hair pulled back into a pony tail. He mentions casually that Jack Bush painted in this studio in the sixties, and talks about the history of artists, not only in this studio, but in this Queen Street West neighbourhood where old warehouse space and low rents made it a good place to paint. The neighbourhod was, in fact, only the most recent artistic community in the city, following a line that began with Adelaide Street in the late nineteenth century, to Grenville Street in the twenties and thirties, the Gerrard Village in the forties, and then Yorkville. But now that Alfred Sung and Le Chateau have moved onto Queen Street the rents have skyrocketed. Inside the new shoestore, Fluevogs, a stained-glass panel from a Victorian church allows an appropriated Mary and young Jesus to gaze out blandly at the rite of shopping.

Once again the artists are being pushed on— some to Dupont and Lansdowne and others out of the city. Andy, Stephen, and Michael are holdouts in the neighbourhood.

Andy tells of the moment back in 1975 when he decided to move to Toronto. "I was a figurative painter and there was nothing in Calgary. I thought there were more chances to show in galleries. But there was one definite moment that decided it for me. We wanted to see *The Discreet Charm of the Bourgeoisie* after it won the Academy Award and we went on the third day of its showing in Calgary. But it was already gone— it had lasted two days. That pissed me off."

Andy and Stephen and Michael all talk of how downtown Toronto was a better place to live when they came in the mid-seventies, cheaper and grubbier and funkier. A voice is heard from the stairs (the door is left open so friends can come and go) and a woman comes into the studio, an artist named Sybil Goldstein who shows at the same gallery as the others, Garnet Press. She pours herself a coffee and joins in the talk about how the city has changed for artists trying to live and work.

"Everybody's after the corporate buck," Sybil says.

"In certain ways I've become more practical," says Stephen. "I make smaller works. Every once in a while only do I make a really big work."

Andy says, "You can't live just on sales or just on grants anymore. Nor can you work part-time and survive. It's always a struggle."

"I might claw my way up to the poverty line," Sybil laughs. "That's why there are so many artists leaving the city and going to Flesherton."

"I don't think it's only money," says Michael. "It's getting to be such a rat race, it's so competitive."

All the friends say they love the neighbourhood but complain of how it is being changed by the chain stores moving in, the crowds coming up from the Dome, and the weekend gawkers dressed up in what Andy calls "yuppie boho." Sybil says, "As long as you can still run into people you know it's okay. I was visiting a friend who lives in Forest Hill. They make appointments to see one another. Here we don't have to because we know we're going to meet them anyway, on the street, or at the Stem. Artists are pretty social beings.

Your time and your life are more casual."

When Sybil mentioned Forest Hill she grimaced, and Stephen says, "Hey, I need Forest Hill and Rosedale to skim off some dough." At first I think he's talking about selling his art to people who live there but it turns out he means his summer job cutting lawns. Now they all start talking about how grants have shrunk, rents have risen, and the usual juggle to survive is getting more frantic. And they are at least 'established' artists with a gallery; younger artists coming up behind think they're hogging all the attention. Sybil says, "People will not spend eight hundred dollars on a painting, but they'll drop the same amount in Visa bills for restaurants. And where does that go? In the toilet! People are terrified of making an aesthetic commitment. It's not just a matter of money. It's the fear of making a judgement. So instead they take a course at the ROM and start collecting eighteenth century silver."

"But I like the edge here," Andy says.

Stephen says, "You know what they say— it pushes you to make better art."

Michael: "I couldn't be a video artist in Flesherton." Laughter.

Andy: "Now when they travel, most visual artists wonder, could I live here? Ten years ago if you went to Winnipeg you wouldn't check out the loft space. But when you're away from Toronto you miss the galleries."

Stephen: "The buzz."

Sybil: "Schmoozing!"

Michael (sarcastically): "We love it here!"

Stephen (seriously): "I do. I adore this city."

Andrew: "Chinese food is important."

Sybil (in a Blanche Du Bois voice): "I can't live without my friends!"

A couple of artist friends have wandered up the stairs and put Prince's new *Batman* CD on the player. We all get up from the table and in the dusty light Andy and the newcomers begin to dance.

"IT HAS A FIVE-PIECE with whirlpool," Charles Pachter tells the long-distance caller. "And you're right in the heart of everything— it's like Greenwich Village. We're talking serious centre of the city. The rent is eighteen hundred dollars. John Borman, the director, is in one now. The chief production-designer of *Phantom of the Opera* is in another and he's deliriously happy."

While Charles Pachter is on the phone in the kitchen I wait in the living room that has a baby grand at one end, and is lined with his own paintings. Among the piles of books on the history of the city is an early edition of the *Diary of Mrs. Simcoe*. The house, tucked onto Grange Place near the Art Gallery of Ontario, was a Victorian blacksmith's shop that Charlie, as his friends call him, has completely renovated, and it is the only property remaining from his mini-empire of Queen Street West real estate in the seventies. Since the 1982 recession, when interest rates hit twenty-two percent and nearly wiped him out, Pachter has managed to buy a small building on Beverley Street and turn it into a six-plex.

Charlie enters the room, a sprightly and slightly-rounding man with a neat greying beard. He happily takes me outside to see his Beverley Arms, a small square building painted a dark purple and with modern windows fitted in. He speaks of liking human spaces, gardens, and the influence of the Kyoto style. "I lost it all at age forty," he says of his real-estate holdings. "I had to sell it all for under a million dollars. Now it's worth forty. Maybe it was good for me. I mean, that's what life is all about, isn't it, to succeed to the best of your ability."

As we walk back to the house I ask him about the two sides of his character, entrepreneur and artist, and whether he thinks of them as separate. "It's all the same to me," he says. "The word entrepreneur means making something out of nothing. I've had big losses. But my art has saved me. The other stuff is a way of connecting to the real world. It's temporal. But I never came to terms with the fact that I have a very good business sense. It's that romantic image of the artist as misunderstood and starving in his garret like in *La Bohème*. A lot of artists are programmed to be neurotic. If you're not, if you don't need someone to hold your hand and take care of you, you're no good."

Charlie speaks with a brisk and infectious energy as he describes how he has taken on the art system by becoming his own dealer and showing his work not in prestigious galleries but in popular spaces such as the Ontario Science Scentre. And he dismisses those artists complaining about how Toronto is changing. "The people who grumble the most may turn out not to be very good artists. I am one of the only Canadian artists I know who has never gotten a grant and who has made a living on symbols of this place. What artists have to learn is that true liberation is knowing what the market will bear. And not being embarrassed about doing it. There is something very noble about the marketplace. In our culture people value things through money. I'm known for three images of the hundred or so I've made— the streetcars, the moose, and the flags. An artist has to provide for the culture. Those other images are my inner soul, my struggle and torment, but what Rosedale duchess is going to put one up on her wall? If a buyer comes in and says I like that flag painting but I want the background in blue then I do it in blue. There's this myth about a buyer coming in and wanting a painting to match the sofa. What's wrong with that? If the person is willing to pay ten thousand dollars for it then it's just another form of commission. Where does this pompous elitism come from? Do what the culture is demanding you to do. And you can also do your own art, the indulgent masturbatory stuff."

We go to the dining room table so that Charlie can show me the limited edition of Margaret Atwood's *The Journals of Susanna Moodie* that he designed and as we look through the lithographs on the table he tells me of his own interest in Toronto, an interest that has skipped past his own Jewish-immigrant ancestry (he was born on Palmerston, the son of a man who was variously a jobber, a "deskman" at a brokerage house, and in the *shmate* business) to its British origins. Why he should have become so fascinated Charlie can't say. "Very few become interested in the history of the city like I did. I think we take it for granted that we'll teach the masses everything. But the masses are Kentucky Fried, the masses are Mosport. When I read about Mrs. Simcoe schlepping up here in 1793 I think, what a woman of courage. It was like a fucking Eden when they got here. She writes about them using birch bark to scoop fish out of the Don River."

Perhaps his own impulse for self-reliance has given Charlie a sense of kinship with the early pioneers of Toronto. As for the changes now, he believes them to be a natural process of urban maturation. He tells me of the fight he had over his own Beverley Arms; the city government and neighbourhood groups worried that the upscale renovation would cause rents to rise in the neighbourhood. "Why not build something beautiful that people from all over the world can live in and enjoy?" he asks. "There's a happy balance in letting those who can do prosper and in taking care of those who can't." He waves vaguely north, towards Chinatown. "Do the Chinese know from welfare?"

When I mention that the poverty in the city is worsening, Charlie sighs. "Here's a story for you, a typical Toronto story. I was making supper the other night and went to the front porch to take out the garbage. But I couldn't open the door because there was a wino fast asleep on the step. To be honest I recoiled because he was covered in flies and stinky. So I phoned the police. And the woman says, 'Is it an emergency?' I say, 'I don't know, he's just lying there.' So she says, 'I can't send a car unless it's an emergency.' 'All right,' I say, 'It's an emergency.' When the policeman comes he's very gentle, he just prods the wino with his nightstick and tells him to sleep in the park. I'm wondering, should I give the guy a meal or ten bucks? But the policeman says he'll just use it to drink that barber's stuff. I'm a bleeding heart liberal and the policeman is telling me to forget it. I honestly think that if a person wants to get better he will— with help. It doesn't make you feel any better that someone would allow himself to fall so low."

Before I leave, Charlie takes me around the house to see his works. Among them are a few of the infamous moose and queen paintings as well as one of the Canadian flag canvases that have been a popular success but sneered at by the critics. I had seen three of these large canvases already, in the lobby of the Stock Exchange Tower, and was struck by how perfect they looked there.

Charlie and I stand on the sidewalk at the side of his house, the green of his roof garden just visible above. "Here I am," he says wonderingly, "a native Jewish Toronto boy living in the heart of Chinatown, across from the AGO which is my temple. I can go and stand before Titian, I can go for dim sum or browse in the bookstores on Queen Street. And I can still go to Switzers for a corned beef sandwich, although I suspect that won't last long."

EGLINTON AVENUE, between Marlee and Oakwood, is a much denser black neighbourhood than I realized. Young men, some with dreadlocks but most without, hail each other on corners as reggae music drifts from cars. In a barber shop a mother is watching her son get his hair clipped down to the scalp by a barber in a white smock. The streetscape of two and three storey buildings of dull brick is drab but human in scale. Most of the businesses here are owned by blacks— the record stores and Jamaican patty places, restaurants with such names as Mr. Jerk and Supreme. On the telephone poles posters advertise an upcoming gospel concert at the West-End Church of God of Prophesy.

Not surprisingly, Clifton Joseph hasn't arrived yet at Spence's. He is hard to get on the phone and didn't make it to our first meeting, due, he said, to his life going "topsy-turvey." But I suspect that Clifton has a looser and easier sense of time that frustrates those of us who live by our watches. I buy a pineapple drink and wait.

Spence's is in a low strip of shops whose white-brick facade looks as if it dates from the fifties. The food is cooked up front where it's warm and steamy and you take your pick of fry fish or oxtail and then sit at the orange formica tables in the back. Above the pegboard shelves of packaged food is displayed shiny new cricket equipment— bats, balls, shoes, kneepads.

After half an hour Clifton saunters in. "I brought my own juice," he says, pulling a bottle from his bag. He is thirty-two, his kinky hair cut short and tucked under a black leather cap, the little goatee and tortoise-shell sunglasses making him very, very cool. I once saw Clifton perform before a mostly white audience, reciting his street-smart, sometimes polemical, thoroughly enchanting poetry. The poem I remember best was a tribute to Thelonius Monk, a long, bellowing, and finally transcendental jazz-lick. He has been influenced by African folk tales, the Harlem Renaissance, and rap. But Clifton, who emigrated from Antigua in 1973, also has an English degree from York University, and listening to him I thought of what a critic once said of Langston Hughes— that he possessed a cultivated artlessness.

Clifton tells me that he moved into this oldest and largest of the West Indian neighbourhoods about four years ago. "This is the biggest, baddest black business area for sure," he says. He has a resonant voice and a deep infectious laugh. I ask whether there are many differences among West Indians here, depending on their place of origin. Most are from Jamaica, Cliff says, but all are influenced by the language of their colonial past, Dutch, Spanish, English, French. Some of the food is different— the Guyanese eat shark, the Jamaicans oxtail. "Basically we're African people," he says. "We see ourselves as one. In the culture, especially my generation and after, people are more interested in the expression of the cultural experience here."

We talk about the establishment black community, those who have done well in Toronto. "There are black businessmen making big dollars"— and to prove his point he motions to the next table where a man in a grey suit is eating his lunch, a cellular phone standing on the formica table by his elbow. I ask whether the successful support the rest of the community, especially the artists struggling to get known. "Some of them do, but really and truly most of them don't," he says. "Of course, these people might be from a different class to begin with and that difference gets highly glossed over. Some have done well through underhanded means like most businessmen, and some through genuine achievement. Nursing homes, record stores. The black middle class will get involved in certain issues like race relations and affirmative action. Even the black property class gets upset over police brutality.

"Toronto has not resolved the issue of colour," Clifton says. "Here the cops might shoot you, might pick you up. There are teenage kids who have a string of arrests already. You might have a cousin or an uncle who has been beaten up by the police. If you go like this"— he pretends to bump against me— "that's 'resisting arrest.'" I remark that a perception exists among many people that drugs and crime are worsening in the city and that black kids are heavily responsible. Clifton answers carefully: he wants to note clearly his own concern for these problems. "Inside the black community, like inside the Italian, WASP, and Jewish communities, there is a criminal element. Hey, we know who's bringing the drugs in," he says, alluding to organized crime in Colombia and to the Iran-Contra scandal. "Here in Toronto we have the militarization of the situation, throwing gasoline on fire, instead of stopping the big guns. The police use the pretext of drugs to harass the black community. It's a question of the selectivity of the crime fighting. Is this where the big money is made?" Clifton disparages "Jack and Jill White Guy," who support the police no matter what by pointing up the danger of the job. "I was working once putting up fiberglass in buildings," he says. "Shit, that was dangerous work, man. Everybody takes risks. Some people in this town are sleepwalking."

To Clifton, police behaviour is just one manifestation of the racism that blacks face in Toronto, along with employment, housing, and the arts. The "streaming" of kids in the school system to higher and lower levels, he claims, steers black kids away from university. And the ascendency of the black middle class is not compensation. He expresses an historical consciousness that spans not only time but borders. "We were brought over here in chains and it's the same system that has evolved into late twentieth century capitalism. When we call for changes we don't just mean more middle class jobs. Not that that shouldn't happen. We're one of the most educated groups in this city. You ought to see the degrees and shit some of these guys got and they still can't get a job. Listen, you have to deal with the man's system every day. We need independence and you can use capitalist elements to get that. But I'm talking about socialism, cooperative ventures. In some ways we've got a very politicized community— a lot of people are involved with the politics of their homelands. But sometimes local issues aren't as high on the political agenda. Right now, though, we're going through a nationalist surge— anti-systems, anti-capitalist. Particularly with the young people. They're more identified with Africa and especially with radical culture."

I ask Clifton about this surge of interest in Africa from people who were not born there and most of whom have never visited. On the streets I see African symbols on leather medallions and on T-shirts sporting the red, black and green of black liberation. Clifton explains it by talking about the white's early need to justify slavery— "By claiming the inferiority of the African, nigger, coon, Aunt Jemima. So now we're going through a re-invigoration of African consciousness. Man, I mean the Moors built the universities in Spain, there was Hannibal"— and he names several other African historical events. "We know that man originated in Africa— that's a historical fact. America is two hundred years old. That ain't shit! We're talking about Africa, the biggest continent, that gave genesis to humans. Look east! So in our minds Africa becomes a looming giant. We were taken from there. It is a heavy romance. We're claiming the African past. It's one of those psychic things. Africa." He makes the word ring.

Clifton himself knows that Africa has a complicated history of achievement, colonialism, and failure. Yet he recognizes the moral and psychological power the continent can have and that the first step in the improvement of the blacks' condition is a sense of pride. After that must come organization. "Otherwise it'll just evaporate. So we can fight the system when it messes with us. We've been here a long time. Black folks have helped build this city and make it vibrant. We demand due respect and treatment like everybody else. Or some mother fucker has got to pay. Tomorrow is too late. As Malcolm X said, by all means necessary. The problem with the system is that it's a big bad monstrous animal. It knows how to cool you out. We've had people working in the system for a decade and things have just got worse. How long do we have to wait? Langston Hughes asked that in a poem—

What happens to a dream deferred?

Does it dry up
like a raisin in the sun?
Or fester like a sore—
And then run?
Does it stink like rotten meat?
Or crust and sugar over
like a syrupy sweet?
Maybe it just sags
like a heavy load
Or does it explode?"

Clifton laughs heartily. "That shit was written in 1925, man."
When Clifton makes these ambigious threats, his voice is not brutal

but strangely poetic. I heard that edge before, when Clifton performed before the white audience. He made the audience first laugh and then shift uncomfortably with his talk of black people taking over the city. And then followed his deep laugh that we didn't know if we should join. So I ask Clifton about that— about the poetically-phrased threat.

He tells me how he started to recite poetry when still a child in Antigua. Then he began to write his own, adding a congo drum and flute player. His work now, he says, is different from the didactic political verse of his youth. "I'm an artist, dig, a stylist," he says. "I want to maintain poetry as a performance art. There's a bag of tricks that comes from story-telling and black vocal style. The ease with which I can get my point across to you depends on my technique. Sometimes I use a soft technique, sometimes an arrogant technique. And sometimes I put you on edge. Talking about the black takeover. I just do that to unsettle the white audience. Ha! And a lot of black audiences too. I've been banned from performing at one school for reciting a poem called "Pimps." And another for taking out a knife. But sometimes artists are so aestheticized." He hisses the word. "The audience might just give you the patronising clap. Clap-trap. I want to establish a groove where I can put you through where I am. I'm perfectly willing to go with something and an audience won't get it until next year. I need to get people up a little. I'll deliberately frighten a couple of people in the front row."

He demonstrates by biting out the first word of a poem, lunging towards me so that I jerk back. "At least they won't slouch! That's why Shakespeare's opening scenes are so tumultuous— you have to stop that chatter around you. There are some white people who come to hear me who don't like what I say but like the way I say it. They've got the two sides of themselves warring. I can use that groove, that's all right with me. Maybe one side will start to understand the other."

Cliff decides that we've sat long enough in one restaurant without spending and so we shift next door to a fast-food place called Rap's where the day's specials are cowfoot, stewbeef, and steamed fish. He tells me about the record album that he's producing independently and how the release has been delayed by a lack of cash. Because he and his fellow dub poets, as the style is called, are misunderstood even by the mainstream arts community, they have had to learn to publish themselves. "We're more than poets," he says. "We're producers, hucksters, promotion wizards. It has strengthened us. It also wears the shit out of you."

Clifton waves down a man in a leisure suit passing the restaurant and the two sit at another table for a few minutes, looking through some papers. Returning, Clifton says that the man is one of the local producers he works for, promoting their theatrical productions brought in from Jamaica. I ask if this is Clifton's usual way of doing business and he nods. "I'm not in a normal time frame at all." And then he starts to talk about Toronto, praising the city's night life. "It's a big town now. At the same time, it's taken a turn for the worse. And just look at all those big projects. They said the money from the new Convention Centre would trickle down to me. It hasn't happened yet, something is wrong with the pipes, man," he chuckles. "The developers have dug in deep and vicious. This city is self-satisfied, smug, jive, two-faced and fork-tongued. There are times when I wake up like today, saying this place is a real mother fucker. Look at Patricia Starr, at the municipal election campaigns funded by developers. Just yesterday I was on Bay Street for the first time in a long while. I couldn't believe how it had changed. Marble buildings, condos and shit. The rich have basically taken over the town. And we're going to see more woe for the poor. The shit hasn't hit bottom yet."

From the table, Clifton greets a woman friend behind the restaurant counter, and the two begin a friendly argument over the Spike Lee movie, *Do the Right Thing*. In the movie an angry crowd of blacks burns down an Italian pizza parlour in their Brooklyn neighbourhood. The woman, who is white, didn't like it. But Clifton admires the movie and sensitively analyzes the motivations of the characters and the way the film maker "deconstructs the film process." And as for the violent climax, he looks through his dark tortoise-shell glasses and puts on his mysterious half-smile. "They should have burned down all of fucking New York."

We say goodbye on the street. A couple of Clifton's friends who were standing at the corner are already approaching. Clifton shakes my hand with a wiggling motion. "That's cool, man," he says.

ON THE VIDEO screen a woman's naked torso moves back and forth. *I'm on fire. What has set me on fire?* From the sofa two women watch and smoke as other women cross the screen, moving from one room to another. The video cuts to a scene of two women drinking beer at a kitchen table. *I had always understood what it felt to be marginalized. It was difficult to face my blind spots in other areas...*
Carla Murray, a tense-looking woman— or perhaps it's just nervousness over this open house— tells me why she helped found the Women's Art Resource Centre on College Street. In art school she had asked why none of the classes were taught by women. "Because there are no women artists," the administrator had told her. Now the centre has three hundred members whose work it supports and documents.
I return to watch the compilation of videos. The screen flashes the name of the next work— *Vulva Performance*— and a woman appears, dressed in a latex costume that clumsily represents the female sexual organ. The women on the sofa laugh. I wonder how many people— or rather how few— will ever see these videos which bore one moment and surprise the next. Yet they are a part of the alternative ways of viewing the world that the city shows us. Their pleasures and discomforts are one of the compensations and challenges of living here. Lately it has seemed to me that the city and art are merging, so that the two become indistinguishable. The other morning, before most of the city was awake, I had seen coffins, wrapped in plastic like giant candies, being unloaded from a truck and carried into the McDougall and Brown Funeral Home on St. Clair. Later that day, walking by an optician's window on College Street, I saw that it had been turned into a little exhibition space. Behind the glass were six exquisitely made coffins, each the size of a shoebox, and resting in each an old microphone. The text on a card read: *These miniature coffins, each housing a disfunctional microphone, represent the death of language...*
Just this week I walked into the Art Gallery of Ontario on a whim. And stood before two works in a show of European artists, beside an elderly couple who shook their heads at what was passing as

art these days. And while I couldn't blame them, both works had a strange effect on me. The first, by an Italian named Michelangelo Pistoretto, was called "The Orchestra of Rags." It consisted of seven piles of rags, each topped by a square of glass. To the couple it looked like mere rubbish, but I immediately thought of the old woman who lives in front of Trinity-St. Paul's Church on Bloor Street, surrounded by her bags and bundles. The work looked to me like a village of the homeless.

The second work, by Bertrand Lairer of France, required even fewer of the usual artistic skills. The artist had simply set a refrigerator atop a safe. Really, it was outrageous— how could anyone pay money for such a thing? But seeing it, I laughed aloud, for just that week I had visited a new house in Forest Hill. And the most impressive attributes of the house were its enormous refrigerator and a safe in the basement.

The voice drones from the video. *The question we now have to ask is whose voices are absent?*

Mrs. God's Wounds

IN THE FINANCIAL district of King and Bay the noise of construction is deafening. Gears, jack hammers, crashing balls, screeching cranes, the shouts of men. Between the pure modernist towers of the TD Centre, the golden tiers of the Royal Bank, the white rectangle of First Canadian Place, the new buildings are being shoehorned in: BCE Place, 100 Yonge, the Yonge Richmond Centre, Bramalea's One Queen East. On the fourth storey of the skeleton structure of One Financial Place a workman in a yellow hardhat steps along a narrow beam. He pauses, balances there above the street, and waves down at a woman in a blue dress who has looked up towards him.

This latest frenzy of construction exceeds that first burst of skyscraper-building from 1922 to 1927, when fourteen went up. Nineteen twenty-nine brought the thirty-four storey Bank of Commerce, the tallest in the British Empire and still the most handsome in Toronto. That is the paradox of the cityscape; down on the ground a nightmare of oppressive tunnel-streets, and inside airless offices floating as if unconnected to the planet. But from afar the skyline turns beautiful; a mythical enchanted city.

The National Bank Building on York Street is one of the least notable towers in the district: anonymous glass walls, anonymous waterfall. Nor does Blott Fejer Felkai Rovet have one of the more glamorous law offices downtown. It has no winding staircase like Tory Tory DesLauriers and Binnington; its walls are not hung with

70

Louis de Niverville, Molinari, and Brian Boigon like McCarthy and McCarthy. But Allan Blott is one of the most influential development lawyers in town, and the work has made him rich. Before the last election, Allan Blott was reported to have sat in on city council meetings, nodding to certain councillors at the times of votes. As a fundraiser he has flushed out large sums for these same councillors' political campaigns, turning around to lobby them on behalf of his clients, moving forward approvals for condominium and office projects that exceed the official plan.

Allan Blott has not yet returned from a meeting, so I sink into a sectional leather couch and gaze through the glass doors to the hallway. It was at another forum that I first saw him, debating with John Sewell, the former reform mayor who had just been removed from his position as head of the Metropolitan Toronto Housing Authority. Sewell, who had obviously lost his faith in local government and now considered it obstructionist, called on public housing groups, concerned citizens, and private developers to solve the housing crisis. Blott took a different tack. He said that we can view our city three ways: as a city of neighbourhoods, as a provincial centre, or as a world class city. To be honest, the idea of a city of neighbourhoods seemed so much more appealing that I was suprised to hear Blott call for us to grasp the great opportunity before us and become that world class city. Sitting here waiting for him now his words sound similar to those of Robert Bandeen's more eloquent talk of "international excellence." The term "world class," so vague in its meaning, has a strange objectifying effect; it tells us to judge and define our city not with our own eyes but through the eyes of outsiders, to look at ourselves in somebody else's mirror. But Blott's use of "world class" also surprised me because it has been so discredited lately, and is now a term of irony. Even the politicians and developers who bandied it around so freely when promoting the Skydome have quietly dropped it from their rhetorical vocabulary.

Now through the glass doors a woman enters, with a stylishly short haircut and the most elegant maternity dress I've ever seen. When she says my name I look again and recognize her as a former classmate from York Mills Collegiate. Now she's an associate lawyer at Blott Fejer and is expecting her first child. "I'm taking off as long as I legally can," she says. "Four months." Will she bring the baby into the office? I ask. "Oh yeah," she says, and rolls her eyes.

Watching my old schoolmate disappear down the hall, I'm reminded of a young man named Elliott Lefko whom I had gone to see. Elliott is one of the most risk-taking music promoters in the city, booking radical bands into venues such as the Apocalypse Club. But when I met him in his junior one-bedroom apartment on St. George, he looked like the guys I'd hung around with in high school, guys who were crazy about astronomy and Monty Python. Elliott, despite his reputation on the music scene, leads an economically marginal life. His few pieces of furniture are out of date and battered, his stereo is old, and the green rugs on the floor look like carpet remnants. Elliott doesn't own many records anymore; he has sold them off during tight times. What stayed with me after our talk was not the ideas about music, but Elliott's somber look when I asked how it felt to run into friends from high school who were now lawyers or in business. "It's a good point," he said quietly. "I see people I went to school with wearing suits. I've lost those kinds of things— a house, vacations in Jamaica. But I've gained other things. This has kept me young." And though he sounded sincere, his voice never lost its dark tone.

Allan Blott swings through the glass doors, pauses at the receptionist's desk, and then breezes past. A few moments later I am ushered into his office to find him hunched over a Greek salad in a take-out container— at three o'clock he is just finding time for lunch. Mr. Blott gets his questions off first: why am I writing this book? Who else have I spoken to? They are legitimate questions, though none of the low income people or community workers have ever asked them. Mr. Blott has steely eyes and an unsmiling demeanour. I ask about the new reform council that has presumably blown away some of his influence.

"There's so little that they can do in the time that's allotted to them," he shrugs, spearing a piece of cucumber. It's true, he says, that the council can stall some projects, but the lifespan of reform politicians in municipal politics is short, and in the meantime the developers will wait patiently. In the end, he asserts offhandedly, the marketplace always wins out.

But surely the voters expressed their disgust by ousting so many pro-development councillors and the "let's make a deal" style of land-use tradeoffs whereby high densities are allowed in return for other concessions. "I don't get excited about short-term reaction to anything anymore," he says. "I remember twenty years ago the short term reaction to St. James Town. How dense it was. Nobody likes the three buildings that Huang and Danczkay built," he says, referring to the worst Harbourfront highrises. "But nobody liked it there before the buildings. Ten years from now, if east of Yonge Street is developed, will everybody say, 'I can remember when you could walk among the shacks there?'"

Mr. Blott warms to his subject. He tells how the government is up in arms against the not-in-my-backyard syndrome, or NIMBY. While everybody thinks that affordable housing is a good idea, nobody wants it next door, believing that property values will sink in spite of studies that show otherwise. So the government wants to ignore neighbourhood opinion on these projects and then turn around and call itself populist by blocking downtown condominium towers. After all, Allan Blott says, condominiums are housing too, but government either uses or ignores public opinion depending on its own wishes. Simple hypocrisy. And to his mind, reformers have often hurt the city. Look at the halting of the Spadina Expressway, he says. That benefited only a few people who didn't want their neighbourhood to change, and now the traffic is disastrous and manufacturers are moving out because they can't get their trucks in and out of the city.

I remind him of John Sewell's call for non-profit housing groups and private developers to join together to solve the housing crisis. "They do already, they've been doing that for years," Allan Blott says, and of course he's right. The current provincial government Homes Now program funds just such projects, but it will soon run out. "That whole phenomenon is a result of allocation, by the feds or the province. By and large those allocations get used up. I don't see how all of a sudden that's going to double. I don't see more developers getting into the act. They never have to beat the bushes to find developers for these projects."

So the supply of affordable housing will always remain inadequate, according to Allan Blott. I ask whether he believes there is any way of helping not only low-income people but middle class familes who can no longer buy homes here. But he says these families are out of luck. "I think as a society we can only look after the needy," he says. "You've now moved into the stratosphere above. Look what it did to New York."

As I get up to leave, Mr. Blott is already instructing his secretary to arrange a conference call. Down on King Street the daytime bustle has turned to rush hour frenzy. Allan Blott does not strike me as a likeable man, but he was forthcoming in his opinions and something he said rings in my mind as I am jostled by men in dark suits and women tripping on their heels.

"It's never going to change."

THE RECEPTIONIST at Deloitte Haskins and Sells informs me that Gordon Riehl is not in. Mr. Riehl, a Deloitte partner, is at the Board of Trade's offices in First Canadian Place.

I take the elevator down the thirteen storeys, cross the TD Centre's plaza, enter the pillared lobby of the Board of Trade, and take the elevator up to the fourth floor. The receptionist, wearing a headset like an airport traffic controller, informs me that Mr. Riehl is at Deloitte Haskins and Sells.

"But I was just there," I pant.

After several phone calls a secretary is sent through the offices of the Board to look for Mr. Riehl, but without success. I sit down to wait and read a profile of Gordon Riehl published in the Board's magazine. Mr. Riehl has just become president of the Board of Trade of Metropolitan Toronto, making him (in the words of the article) the "spokesman for almost sixteen thousand senior businessmen." The article carries a sidebar describing the president's forty-three foot Richardson cabin cruiser that sleeps eight and is moored between Ontario Place and Exhibition Stadium. But I'm more interested in its description of Mr. Riehl as a "civic minded advocate for the business community." Certainly the business community contributes positively to Toronto and Mr. Riehl must have some ideas on the matter. After all, the Board's own authorized history is called *To Serve the Community.*

The secretary calls me to the telephone; Mr. Riehl is on the other end. Apparently there was a mix-up, but if I wouldn't mind waiting a little longer he will gladly take me to lunch.

I sit down again, this time picking up the Board's annual report. From its Victorian beginnings, the Board has tried to influence the direction of the city's progress, and the report shows the Board just as eager to do so now, for it has made dozens of submissions to all levels of government in the past year. The one that catches my eye is on housing; the Board has proclaimed its opposition to the Ontario Ministry of Housing's requirement that twenty-five percent of all new housing be affordable. The term "affordable" is not as restrictive as it might sound; such housing must be within reach of households earning up to fifty-eight thousand dollars a year. Nevertheless, the Board considers the rule an "unnecessary interference in the housing market."

When Gordon Riehl arrives, he looks older and a little more stiff than I expected from his photograph in the magazine, but his long face is tanned and fit. He wears a modest blazer, although his shirts, as he mentions in passing, are custom made. We sit down in the bar adjacent to the Board's private dining room where Mr. Riehl calls the waiter by his name, John. After he orders the shrimp fettuccini, I ask Mr. Riehl about that civic-mindedness.

"You ought to read about the history of the Board," he says. "It started in 1845, at least that's in recorded history. The business community of the city has always taken more than just a business interest. A hundred years ago it was working to create more parks. Besides, business people don't just work here; they live here too, so they can be concerned from a selfish point of view."

Mr. Riehl is in no hurry to speak and pauses for a long moment. "Take for example housing. Right now there's a shortage of help in the city. Manpower. We want to see that cured and our point of view is that the government got into tinkering with the law of supply and demand and monumentally screwed up. Now they don't have the political will to get out of it. We'd like to see good, affordable rental housing in the city. But nobody will build rental housing with rent control on. And the other thing is the lack of services for developing land. City Hall creates so much red tape you'd think it's their job to prevent subdivisions."

I mention assisted housing and he says, "We know there are people who need subsidies and we think they should get them." But some critics, I suggest, think the government isn't spending enough money on building new subsidized housing. He pauses for a full minute. "If the government does, it means using tax money that might mean they can't make more parks or fix roads." He pauses again. "So there'll be potholes."

Mr. Riehl listens as I wonder aloud about working people and even middle-income families who can neither qualify for subsidies nor afford Toronto house prices. He says, "Our position is that the government should do what people can't— schools, roads, sewers. They've never had to get into the housing market until recently and there's really no need for that." As he seems to be ignoring the high cost of housing in the city, I mention the current idea that builders be encouraged to put up smaller homes more densely to allow for more people and lower prices.

"Do you agree with that?" he peers at me.

"It sounds like a good idea."

"Well, I'm a little concerned about it. Do we pack people in so that we become a kind of Calcutta?" He laughs. Certainly big houses and large back yards are nice, I suggest, but what if people can't afford them? "I think if we do that we'll need more open spaces," he says. "I think we should be careful that we just don't overdo it."

Mr. Riehl begins to reminisce about how Toronto has changed. "It's a much more exciting place than it was," he says. "When I was young we used to think an exciting city was always in America. Now American friends come here and think it's terrific." He tells of frequent visits to the O'Keefe and the Royal Alexandra. "My wife loved *Cats*," he chuckles. "She went to see it four times." Jokingly, I say that I had thought business people were too busy to go out for pleasure. "Oh, I see an awful lot of them there," he says, and mentions the many businessmen who have contributed financially to the arts in the city, such as Kenneth Thomson, who paid for Roy Thomson Hall. But I remember that while the Thomson family did donate four and a half million dollars, that was less than what the taxpayers put in, and a lot of people were angry at the choice of name.

Another businessman Mr. Riehl mentions is Hal Jackman, who controls Victoria and Grey Trust and several insurance companies. Mr. Jackman is heading the drive for the proposed ballet/opera house. "That will make us one of the premier opera cities, won't it?" he asks, as if for my opinion. I tell him of the opposition by groups calling for affordable housing on the site. "If you want to be a first-class city you have to have first class facilities," he says. "I don't want to see anybody not have housing, but if you always had that as an excuse you'd never get anything else built. Toronto would be a cultural wasteland." He pauses and then says mildly, "I think if you let them build the opera house, they're pretty good-intentioned people and they'll turn their attention to something else."

John, the waiter, pours us coffee. I tell Mr. Riehl that one of the impulses behind my talking to people about the city was seeing so many beggars on the street, sometimes four or five within a couple of blocks. Mr. Riehl curiously asks where that is. "That's a phenomenon I've been wondering about too," he says. "Because our unemployment rate is under four percent. So they must be derilects coming from outside the city who don't want to work and think the pickings are better here." But many of the beggars, I say, are teenagers, and Mr. Riehl shakes his head in either wonderment or disgust. "Look at McDonald's," he says, "at signs for sales clerks in the stores. There's no problem getting a job." It's true, I say, that many kids come to Toronto thinking that Yonge Street is paved with gold, but often they are fleeing abusive family situations. Their hard upbringings and lack of education perhaps make them feel as if they have no future and that all that's available for them are service-sector positions, or "McJobs."

Mr. Riehl takes one of his pauses. "One of the fellows I work with is helping to set up a hostel on Wellesley for kids. Give them a place to live so they can get on their feet. But often they fail and he says exactly what you're saying— that they think Toronto is paved with gold."

I listen to Mr. Riehl with a kind of shock. He has responded only to the part he wanted to; as for the rest, it was as if I hadn't said it.

John brings us the chit. "Can I get that?" I ask.

"Are you a member of the Board?" Mr. Riehl says.

"No, I'm not."

"Then you can't."

He signs the chit and we sit over our coffees. Mr. Riehl says, "Somebody's got to do some of those jobs we call dead end, don't they?" And falls silent again.

FOUR-YEAR-OLD Tanya looks up at me suspiciously from washing her doll's hair in the plastic pool. "Who's that?" she asks Karen Thorpe. Karen is the director of the Centro-Clinton Daycare Centre. As we walk through the daycare's bright and chaotic rooms on the first floor of the Clinton Street Public School, children rush up to cling to Karen's legs. One little boy is playing seriously at the indoor sandbox, his trousers and underpants around his knees. "Did you go to the toilet all by yourself?" Karen asks, yanking them up. "Right on!"

The daycare workers at Centro-Clinton are doing one of those jobs that has to be done— taking care of the children. A daycare is a good place to think about the hierarchical values that society places on work. Most of the workers here, having received recent increases, are paid twenty-four to twenty-seven thousand dollars a year. The low salaries mean that daycares have a hard time holding on to their staff. Karen Thorpe believes that society has not fully come to terms with the importance that daycare has in children's lives, now that there are so many single-parent and two-income families. Right now the waiting list for subsidized spaces in Toronto stands at five thousand, but no new spaces are being created.

I first visited Karen at the the co-operative house on Vermont Avenue where she and her sixteen-year-old daughter live. Vermont is a quiet street and the house, of three-storey painted brick, has hardwood floors, deep green walls, and charming, if inexpensive, furniture. After fifteen years of daycare work, Karen still cannot afford a home of her own. "I've seen a lot of good people leave the field," she told me. "I don't know many who have persisted as long as me at the grass roots level. It's a very physically demanding job. Imagine pulling on eight snow suits! And it's a tremendous responsibility because young children are so accident prone. But the work is undervalued because men don't understand— they think women come naturally to taking care of kids. So the workers get demoralized. In my centre they're getting increasingly angry, and for the first time they've asked the parents to form a lobby group and parents are starting to react. I myself have suffered economically, that's for sure. But asking for more money is a tricky emotional thing. If we go on strike, what happens to all those single mothers who have to get to work? And if we ask for more money, we feel guilty for taking more from the families of the kids. That's why daycare workers have subsidized the system for so long."

But Karen didn't want to talk only about the negatives. "The daycare is a wonderful environment," she said. "There's a lot of joy in a centre that's really well run." It might even be the place for the making of a genuinely tolerant community; at Centro-Clinton there are so many national origins that the staff put up a map with pins in it showing where all the kids had been born.

Walking through the rooms of the daycare centre, where the walls are an exuberant patchwork of paintings, collages, and paper chains, I understand what Karen means by joy. At one low table, three kids wearing smocks are taking pink and blue gooey stuff to smear about with their hands. "Mud, mud, mud," they sing, "mud all day long." To the sound of Rita MacNeil on the record player two small girls are running about in wedding veils and tutus. Chris, a four-year old boy with spina bifida, is laughing as he crawls across the floor to grab Karen's ankle. Karen is right, Chris has a wonderful laugh, and I remember what one of the other kids, as she told me, said about him: "Yeah, we can be friends with Chrissy, even though his head's all squished in."

At the window, some laughing faces are watching the kids in the playground outside— a bigger, better equipped playground than most daycares. Soon Rosa, who Karen calls "our earth mother," will be serving chili con carne for lunch. Not everyone is happy, though; in the toddler room, two boys on their first day are weeping big wet tears as they are comforted by the women workers.

Back in the other room, Tanya is still washing her doll. Looking up at me again through half-closed eyes, she says, "Is that guy in the glasses staying for lunch?"

"AIN'T IT TRUE, Maria, how I give all the women a hard time?"

The waitress just holds the aluminum cup under the milkshake maker.

"Everybody know it. Don't I give all the women a hard time, Maria?"

"I'm busy."

"So just give an answer, Maria. Am I giving you a hard time now... "

On the way to the public meeting of the Bread Not Circuses Coalition in Regent Park, I have stopped for something to eat at the Sip and Bite Restaurant on Parliament Street. It was Lynn, who I first met at the Neighbourhood Information Post, who took me here, and its disintegrating condition immediately depressed me. The peeling wallpaper and holes in the linoleum floor, the fan rattling in the dirty men's room, and the sweet smell of roach killer. But Lynn said she came here because the waitresses tolerated her sitting over an order of french fries and gravy (which she topped with ketchup) without leaving a tip afterwards.

I've come back to see if I will feel more at ease on a second visit. This afternoon I had planned to speak to people at random in the streets, but instead I found myself on the fifth floor of the Metro Reference Library, sitting at one of the oak tables and gazing out at Rosedale Valley and the city receding north. Inside the library I had felt safe from that increasing sense of drowning, as if water were slowly rising above the level of my mouth.

The waitress brings a grilled cheese sandwich. Two women and two little girls come into the diner and head for the booth behind me. "J.J., tell your sister to shut up," says the mother, as the girls scramble over their seats.

"Sharrup," the girl says.

"Get down from that table, you little shit."

The first time I came here, with Lynn, I had also ordered a grilled cheese sandwich, but then I had asked for tomato in it. Lynn had stared silently at me and it wasn't until later that I realized the gulf I had opened between us. To ask for something not usually given, even if that something was two pale slices of tomato, required an assurance of one's place and expectations in the world that Lynn did not have.

That whole meeting had been uncomfortable, perhaps because of the questions about Lynn's upbringing that I asked. At one point she said to me from across the table, "I think friendship is a lot more important than writing, don't you?" and while I nodded in agreement I wondered why she had said it.

The waitress stands by my table. "What kind of danishes do you have?" I ask.

"No kind," she says. "It's just a danish."

The mother in the booth behind is talking to her kids. "I'm going to take you home and beat the shit out of you, just to show how much I love you."

I hear a noise. In the next booth a girl of about two is standing on the seat, steadying herself with a hand and smiling a chocolatey smile at me.

THE MAIN CHAPEL of the church in Regent Park is small and light, the floor newly covered with inexpensive carpeting and at the rear of the altar a cross that, from this distance, appears as two large classroom rulers nailed together. The fifty or so people sitting in the pews ignore the thumping feet of kids in the daycare arranged next door and listen to Michael Shapcott recount the origin of the Bread Not Circuses Coalition. Michael wears his usual baggy jeans with the cuffs rolled up, and a T-shirt from CKLN, the community radio station. Early in 1989 the Roomers Association arranged a meeting with Art Eggleton, the mayor. They presented to him the statistics of rising homelessness and increasing lines at the food banks. Mayor Eggleton assured them that he was already spending more time on hunger and housing issues than on any other. The Roomers didn't believe him and that's when the coalition was born, bringing together anti-poverty, feminist, and disarmament groups, social agencies, organizations of nurses, tenants, and union members, community theatres, and some local politicians.

"In the next ten years we're looking at a spending spree on megaprojects," Michael Shapcott says— three hundred million dollars worth, while in the meantime no new federal, provincial, or city funds have been marked for daycare. And these projects, despite being packaged by public corporations, are cloaked in a secrecy that makes information about them impossible to obtain. Bread Not

Circuses wants an open process so that the public can really see where its money is being spent. Michael has the speaker's ability to strip a subject down to its most forceful essentials. While the corporate sponsors behind projects such as the Skydome and the bids for the 1996 Olympics and Expo 2000 are almost identical, he says, the organizers insist that they are unrelated. The advisory committee for the Olympics is made up of businessmen, politicians, and a few athletes, but includes no members of the public, no social workers, no representatives of the neighbourhoods that will be most affected. "The most radical thing is a long memory," Michael says, and he recounts horror stories from previous Olympics and fairs—how the city of Montreal put up painted hoardings to hide the poor districts; how during the Vancouver Expo old men were kicked out of their rooming houses to make way for tourists and several died in the winter streets; how the apartments in Seoul's Olympic Village were sold off as condominiums.

A woman sitting among the speakers gets up. Penny McCabe is a member of the Parkdale Tenants Association. If Expo 2000 is built on the waterfront just south of Parkdale as planned, she says, it will disrupt for six months an already beleaguered neighbourhood. She holds up a hardcover book that has been produced by the fair's sponsors and indignantly reads aloud the caption to a photograph. *Gentrification in Parkdale has made parts of a plain neighbourhood pretty.* That plain neighbourhood is where Penny McCabe lives as well as a lot of others who can't afford other parts of the city. Already, bachelorette apartment houses are being white-painted as a home to ten people becomes a home for a single family. "They may have been illegal, but people were housed," she says.

Carmel Hili, the CRC worker, gets up. In his soft and nervous voice he announces the coalition's plan for a popular culture festival that will show opposition to the ballet opera house to be built at Bay and Wellesley, on land that could be used for affordable housing. Hands shoot up in the audience and people rise to make enthusiastic suggestions for the festival. Then a woman in owlish glasses gets up. "I have to admit that I'm not happy about housing going up before everything," she says. "We ought to have entertainment and the arts too. But how can a family, even a middle-class family these days, go to the ROM or the zoo? The ticket prices are so high they keep people out."

Next to get up is George Dymny, a singer and guitar player who is introduced as a member of the Wobblies, a radical worker's union I thought had died years ago. George Dymny is a gaunt man with a drooping moustache and his voice is rough.

And where will I go,
and where will I stay,
they knocked down skid row
and hauled it away.

"May I just say something?" calls out the woman next to me. I had noticed her earlier because of the young boy on her lap who had run into the daycare, and because of her intense blue eyes. Now she begins to tell her own story, almost obsessively, and it is clear she has been waiting for this moment. Several months ago she went off family benefits to go back to work, only to find herself worse off than before. Now that she earns eighteen thousand dollars a year her rent in a Cityhome apartment has doubled, and expenses like prescription medicine are no longer covered. "I want to be independent," she says. "But I can't afford to work."

A woman sitting in a pew across the aisle stands up to agree. She too is a single mother and tells her own confusing story about the chronic diarrhea that prevents her from working. The women have sidetracked the meeting, but the audience and the speakers nod sympathetically. Michael Shapcott tells of a woman who was told by her welfare officer that her telephone was an unnecessary luxury, even though the woman needed to phone the hospital where her son frequently had to stay for treatment of a heart defect. That woman's telephone is a luxury, he says, but the opera house, the Olympics, Expo 2000— these are "necessities" that demand millions in public money.

George Dymny gets up to sing. "Is Jack here?" he asks, and as if it were planned, Jack Layton, the city councillor who is a supporter of the coalition, enters the chapel. "Good," George Dymny says. "Here's a song about how you can't trust politicians."

Someone shouts, "You can trust this one."

"Well, we always have to watch what they're doing."

And after George sings his cynical tune, Jack Layton comes up to speak. As he talks he is periodically interrupted by fervent applause. Listening, I am reminded of something that Vaclav Havel, the dissident Czech playwright, wrote recently. He was on a Prague street when suddenly President Gorbachev, making a state visit, came out of the national theatre. And as people on the street cheered him, the playwright felt overcome by sadness. The people, he thought, always hope that some external force will save them.

The only hands that do not applaud belong to George Dymny, the musician. They are resting quietly in his lap.

LESLEY HANDS me a pair of scissors and I begin to cut the big letters from the sheet of felt. There's something soothing about the softness of felt, the close following of the pencil line, that brings back the concentration of childhood. The letters are for the banner announcing the Masaryk-Cowan Recreation Centre's arts festival, and Lesley, the centre's art director, shows me where to glue them on. Lying on another table is the community quilt that will go on display for the first time, made from squares stitched by families and organizations in Parkdale. As Lesley tells me as she spreads out the quilt, "There are a zillion service agencies in Parkdale."

The recreation centre is a multi-million dollar conversion of an old curling rink, and from the glass windows of the second floor I can see the gym below where mothers and kids are tossing around balls. From a nearby classroom comes the drone of an English-as-a-second-language class—

I am going to the store,
you are going to the store...

— but like most recreation centres this one seems quiet and underused. After hearing Penny McCabe of the Parkdale Tenants Association, I wanted to visit her neighbourhood. Parkdale is one of those areas invisible to those who don't live there, a blank space between the trendy stretch of Queen Street West and High Park.

What I know, or rather have heard, about Parkdale, is that it's full of ex-psychiatric patients. When institutions like the Queen Street Mental Health Centre began releasing patients, many of them settled in Parkdale because it was nearby and the housing was cheap. In the late fifties a redevelopment scheme allowed developers to raise tall apartment buildings here, turning streets such as Jameson Avenue into bowling alleys of high rises. Then the city government changed its mind and rezoned, and the developers turned to the neighbourhood's big Victorian houses. Parkdale had once been a separate village where prosperous Torontonians had built their houses to get away from the dirt and bustle of the city, but almost no one could afford these near-mansions anymore, and the developers had no trouble buying them up cheaply to divide them into bachelorettes, ten or fifteen to a house.

After gluing down my last letter, I say goodbye to Lesley and walk west on Queen Street, Parkdale's main drag, past diners and those discount electronics stores that have popped up all over the city. Despite the one inevitable gourmet food shop, this part of Queen Street still looks like the plain working-class Toronto of thirty years ago.

One store appears much busier than the others, with people going in and out the door as if there were a fire sale. Reaching it, I see not a store but a sort of community room, with knocked-about chairs, several sofas grouped around a colour television, and a make-shift eating area. The community room's name— the Parkdale Activity and Recreation Centre— seems rather grand, but this place is getting far more use than the Masaryk-Cowan. The men and women in polyester shirts and dirty jeans or sweatpants shift around from one seat to another, from the front desk to the television and back again. They aren't people who look "normal," at least as I am used to defining the term; it's the look in the eye or the way the jaw is held that makes them different.

But it is me who feels awkward and exposed here, sitting down on a bench next to a man who is hunched over and gently bobbing. His bottom lip pouts out and his eyes are droopy. Another man walks up to him and says, "This what you wanted, Bobby?" and hands him a stereo speaker with the wires dangling. "Yeah, that's it," Bobby answers and shoves the speaker into his plastic bag.

"Are you good with electronics?" I ask.

"Yeah. I'm making a stereo," Bobby smiles, but a moment later he looks at me sideways, gets up, and moves to a sofa by the television. It is me he does not trust, I am the stranger here. On the flickering television screen a man is running down an empty subway platform. The woman Bobby has sat beside turns to scowl at me. Her sculpted features and grey eyes are austerely beautiful, even with a haircut that looks as if it were done by placing a bowl on her head. A young man has started pacing back and forth before my bench. Like the rest, he has a reason for being here— a room that's claustrophobic, friends to meet, the need of a sandwich. Having none of these reasons, I feel like a spy. How easy it is to peer into the lives of the poor, how impossible for them to avoid intrusion. The wealthy are so much more difficult to watch; their work and their pleasures transpire behind private doors. But the people here have no doubt been studied enough; they want this space for themselves.

"Hey," says the man pacing back and forth. He stops before me, his grimace of anger strangely dislocated, as if he had forgotten what made him mad. "Where'd you get those glasses from?"

I tell him, realizing that my "Oxford" frames alone make me look different here. "They for reading or seeing far?" he asks aggressively, rocking on his heels. "I need glasses." And he starts pacing again.

After a while I begin, if not to feel comfortable, at least to relax. Nobody is going to ask what I'm doing here, nobody is going to challenge me. It is surprising how short a time it takes before this place begins to feel familiar. Conversations are going on around me, about landlords and families and the Blue Jays. From a Woolworths bag a woman pulls a terrycloth jumpsuit bought for her daughter's birthday. An old man with no teeth says to the woman at the desk, "Hey, Thelma, want to hear a joke? Why did the moron go to the lumber yard? To get a board of education."

Outside again, I walk down the lower streets by the lakefront, where Tourist Home signs sway and give the air of a seaside resort gone to seed. Between the run-down houses stand a few that have been sandblasted and painted, but still fewer than in Cabbagetown. I head north again, past Parkdale Collegiate where the students are sitting on the grass and writing autographs into each others' yearbooks.

In a small park children are playing on the swings, watched by their mothers. I sit down on a bench at the other end of which sits a black woman, elderly and of dignified appearance, her legs neatly crossed beneath her summer dress and her hand rubbing thoughtfully at her chin. The grey strands of her hair are pulled neatly back from her forehead. Politely introducing myself, I ask the woman what she thinks of the city. She looks at me with amused eyes that are both sardonic and understanding, and I feel as if she sees right through me.

"It's war-torn," she says mildly.

I am struck by the powerful metaphor. "Do you mean violence?" I ask. "Has anything happened to you?"

"Oh sure," she says. "I get stabbed hundreds of times a day." Another metaphor, or is she making a fool of me? Because her voice is soft I lean over to hear, but she merely looks slyly at me, like a teacher who knows more than her pupil. "I think we met before," she says. "Oh yes, I was trying to help you get back there."

She points up.

"There?" I say.

"To the universe. The best I can tell you, as I told you then, is that you've got to heal your wounds. Only then can you get back to your mother and father who are waiting for you on the other sphere."

I ask her name. "My name, as I think I told you before, is Mrs. Snowdon. Of course that's the name of one of the two royal families in the city. How old am I? Well, that depends if you mean up there or in my human incarnation. Down here I'm sixty years old. Unfortunately, my husband, who of course is Almighty Father God, isn't with me right now. Me? Quite naturally I'm Almighty Mother God. Who else could I be?"

I cannot get over the disparity of her words and the gentle yet penetrating voice, and I feel both like laughing aloud and as if I almost believe her. "To be Almighty Mother God must be a lot of responsibility," I say.

She shrugs one shoulder and waves a hand. "Yes, it is a lot of responsibility. But there's no sense making it worse than it is." She pats her forehead and runs her hand gracefully over her hair. "As Almighty Mother God it's my duty to help heal the wounds of other people so that they can go back to the place they came from. Up there. Of course, this is really my husband's job by rights, but he's wounded too much himself to be of much use to anybody. He's been shot by cursed Moditon bullets. You never heard of that? They make you stupid."

Apparently, Mrs. God— as I have already begun to think of her— is referring to a drug given to psychiatric patients. She begins to tell me of her rather practical difficulties with social agencies, the police, and her difficulties over lack of money— tells me of them with clarity and insight. Then she says, "I've been waiting a month for extra money. My husband sent me ten cheques from overseas, each for ten million dollars. Held up at the post office." She shrugs. "In the meantime, I have my own wounds to deal with which reduce my powers. Oh yes, they're constantly spraying me with acid and shooting me with hair bullets. Even in my room. The only reason they don't do it now is because you're here. I'm sure it'll start again once you're gone."

Mrs. God begins to talk about the neighbourhood; she gives me historic information about the local churches and describes some of her own volunteer work. When she again brings up my need to return "up there" I ask her how I can do so. "First of all," she says, "you have to heal all your wounds. After that the process is a bit complicated, but I can tell you that it involves doing a head-over-heels cartwheel."

"I'm not very good at cartwheels," I say.

"Oh, it doesn't have to be a good one," and she looks at me as if I'm a little dense.

"I hope I'll see you again," I say truthfully.

"Oh, you will," she waves her hand like a favourite aunt who dislikes sentimental farewells. "Say hello to your mother and father when you get back in the universe. They miss you. Remember, be kind to people. Tell your mother and father that I haven't got all my wounds healed yet but I'm working on it."

When I look back, she is still sitting on the bench, one arm draped over the back. My own place has been taken by a man who is muttering to himself. I wonder if Mrs. God is trying to heal his wounds too.

LOWER YONGE STREET at night, the heavy smell of the lake, the shadow of the art-deco postal building. I walk beneath the concrete bridge of the Gardiner and towards the twinkling lights of Harbour Castle, turning east on Queen's Quay. Only at rare moments do I remember that Toronto has grown up from the harbour of a lake; a city that has grappled so awkwardly and naively for its own image, having no mountain to contemplate, no winding river to romanticize, no confining island to concentrate its essence. Instead, it simply spread and still spreads. The lake is too big, it might as well be an ocean, and now at night the immense sheen of black gives off waves of cold below a white moon.

I walk past the Redpath sugar plant, where the old train tracks begin or perhaps end, and up ahead see people getting out of their cars and walking towards the brick building next to the OPP car depot. The entrance is guarded by iron posts linked by chains, behind which stand two burly young men, one wearing on his belt a metal detector. Someone behind me in the line says, "They're checking for guns. What the fuck is this, Montreal?" In front of me leans a woman dressed in vinyl and stockings of candy-apple red. Like sheep we stand for almost an hour. A woman shakes the frills on her cowboy vest, listens to the music thumping inside the building, and moans. "Oh no, I'm missing 'Lola'!"

The line creeps forward and stops. Meanwhile, every so often a gaggle of friends approaches one of the burly men, says a few words, and magically cross the barrier. "I'm on the waiting list at three law schools," says a voice behind me. "I might end up in New Brunswick." Just when I feel sure we'll still be standing here when dawn breaks, the line surges forward, people break into a near run, and we pass the lifted chain and stream into the foyer where full-sized paratroopers are suspended beneath a dissolving airplane. After paying at the window, we make another surge forward, through the doors as the music and the bodies swallow us up, the Beatles eternally singing "Back in the USSR".

Somewhere ahead is the bar, obscured by the swarm that merges into the vast dance floor. This is "Psychedelic Monday" at RPM, one of the hottest dance-club nights of the week. Flashes of long hair, jeans with American stripes down the sides, paisley vests. But this retro-sixties look, this play-act for an era that has been reduced to a style, is sleeker, sexier, and much more expensive than the original, and the psychedelic colours have been mixed with fishnets and tight black bodices, gorgeously sculpted hair and European jeans. It is the past scrubbed clean and packaged; history for amnesiacs.

I manage to buy from the black-leathered female bartender a "dry" beer— which I don't really like, but everyone is drinking it this week— and climb my way past the go-go girl dancing on her platform to one of the steel balconies. Down below is the mass, swirling centrifugally toward an undefined centre and bathed in the blue and red spotlights. Near one side a group is doing the twist and on the balcony across a woman, though surrounded, dances erotically and narcissistically alone. From below, the voices rise up in a low roar, and there is no place where the dancing actually begins or ends. How beautiful it is, the smoke, the horniness, the right brand names, the pulse of the music beating on the nervous system, the strobe freezing the moment as if we are all inside the blurred image of a video and each of us the centre of the frame.

Or maybe we just want to have fun.

Inside the men's room, where the music retreats, a young man is soaking his shoulder-length curls in the sink. He comes up glistening. "Man," he says, "it's hot out there," and dripping, merges again into the mass.

AMONG THE LETTERS in the morning's mail is an envelope with my address in a laboured handwriting. Although it has no return address and I have never seen the handwriting before, a premonition tells me who it is from, and opening the letter and turning to the bottom I confirm that it is from Lynn. She has decided, the letter says, that she doesn't want me to quote her in my book or refer to her in any way. That I have made her feel uneasy with my "snooping" questions and that I am incapable of understanding her life. Then she gives several pages of thoughtful suggestions of whom I ought to speak to and how I ought to conduct my interviews— by asking only previously agreed upon questions. She ends the letter with what she calls the real reason for not wanting to be quoted: "I just don't trust you or like you very much. You seem to be looking for some pathetic and miserable person to relate to, in order to feel better about yourself."

I sit down, feeling ill, the letter in my hand. Some of the personal questions I asked at the Sip and Bite restaurant must have upset her; no doubt she told me some things that she now regrets. But it's obvious that I have, even if unintentionally, disturbed her far more deeply than that, and the real cause seems to be the confused nature of our relationship. From the beginning I made clear to Lynn that it was as a writer that I wanted to speak to her (we were sitting in the council chamber of City Hall) and she agreed, showing visible signs of emotion. But because of our common interest in poetry and, I thought, a natural liking for one another, it was easy to move towards friendship. But I never stopped listening to her as a writer, never made the distinction of journalist and friend in my own mind, as if it were possible to be both. I believed that I could understand her life, certainly at least gain a degree of empathy, and it is only now, reading her letter, that I wonder if even empathy might be a form of exploitation. After all, I'm the one who chooses which of her words to use and where to put them and, therefore, I who ultimately have control.

I write a letter back to Lynn. In it I apologize for asking questions that she considers too personal, but write that I was acting only as a writer trying to understand the background to the way things are. I write that I won't use her name or what she told me about her life, but that I would like to use some of her comments on government and charities that seem valuable to me. I thank her for helping me to consider whether journalists take advantage of people— that I'm grateful. And I assure her that I have never felt sorry for her or considered her an object of pity, that on the contrary she strikes me as a strong-minded, strong-willed and independent person.

Two days later I receive another letter in the same handwriting.

Dear Cary,

Well, I read your letter over five times and I've decided that even though you have not done anything wrong and have behaved very properly and correctly (choke, choke) I don't like you and I don't trust you & I don't want to talk to you or have anything to do with you even.

I just feel while I've gotten you to be honest in writing, your actions are not honest and you cannot be trusted. I feel, also, that I have nothing in common with you in other ways. You are very firmly aligned with the bourgeoisie and the powers that be, and you are going to be very famous and successful and do very well in life, while I am going to starve to death in the gutter no matter how hard I work. And you know why that is? Because I'm nicer than you, that's why! And more honest than you, too.

Yours truly, Lynn

And you know what I hope? I hope you meet some nut or some unhinged person with a screw loose and have your whole life ruined by her.

Jaguars

THE SKYLINE Triumph Hotel has gruesome wine-coloured carpets, heavy glass chandeliers, and a bar called the Cartier Lounge. In one of the meeting rooms members of the Toronto Entrepreneurs Association are manning their displays of patented clothes hangers, LCD games made in Taiwan, and natural soft drinks. They have read *A Book of Five Rings, Think and Grow Rich*, and the biography of Donald Trump. By day they are engineers, mothers, shopkeepers, employees. But by night and on the weekend they are the acolytes of free enterprise, selling more than a product and more than a philosophy.

Matol is a black, suspicious-smelling liquid that comes in a plastic container shaped like a mortar shell. It was invented by an Austrian who combined the extracts of dozens of flowers and weeds. So the dishevelled woman with the German accent tells me, holding up a photograph of the inventor. "How old do you think he is?" she asks.

"Fifty?"

"Eighty. And he's been drinking Matol since he was a young man. Matol has different positive effects on different people. For me, it has helped with my arthritis. But ask Ivan here, he's been using it for three months now."

Ivan has a bulbous nose and a bad toupe. "Matol has helped me to sleep better at night," he nods. "It allows more oxygen to enter the bloodstream. And you know what else? I've had no allergy symptoms this year."

"Try it." The woman hands me a medicinal cup with a small amount of liquid at the bottom. "One lady who tried it broke into a rash. I told her that was good, that the toxins were coming out of her body. But she wouldn't believe me. This product is sold by multi-level marketing. For every person you sign up to sell Matol you get five percent of their sales earnings, direct from the company."

I swallow the black liquid; the bitterness is followed by an immediate pounding of my heart.

"Doesn't taste too good, does it?" the woman says. "I myself haven't made so much money yet, but I have to start working at it full time. The other day I was at the house of a man who made fifty thousand dollars in one month."

A man in a grey suit picks up one of the plastic Matol bottles. "Oh, my mistake," he says. "I used to sell a laxative that came in a bottle just like this."

"Gangbusters! Gangbusters!"

The shouting comes from Daniel Chang, who is rating the sales of his own invention, Swash. "I am conceived in China," Daniel Chang keeps shouting, as if that were his normal speaking level, "born in Hong Kong, raised in Borneo, educated in Canada. I am creating jobs for Brian Mulroney. Jobs, jobs, jobs! My invention is not made in Taiwan, not made in Korea. It's made in Toronto! In Scarborough!"

Mr. Chang appears as if he might leap over the table to grab my lapels. His device for washing golf balls is a white box that clips onto the golf bag. "It took me one year to get Swash on the market which is unheard of!" he bellows. "Cost of a quarter-million dollars. I sold shares, like the guys who started Trivial Pursuit. Now I work fourteen hours a day, seven days a week. I haven't seen a movie for a year. This is my baby. And you know what? I've never played a game of golf in my life. But for twenty years I researched the secrets of success. At first I was interested only in spiritual growth. I studied philosophy, psychology, religion, mysticism, parapsychology, and alchemy. I discovered that when you have the secret of spirituality you can use exactly the same formula for financial success. That formula has six ingredients. Do you want to hear them? One: do you have a clear picture of your goal? Two: do you want it so bad it possesses you? Three: what kind of plan have you got? Four: action. Five: do you believe in yourself? And six: persistence. Keep on kicking, kicking, kicking."

IF DANIEL CHANG kicks hard enough he might kick himself into Rosedale. At the Rosedale station I get off and walk on Crescent Road to Avondale. In the mid-1860s, Rosedale was laid out as a wealthy enclave in the city. No corner stores here; they were outlawed in 1905. The vines spread over stone walls, walkways meander up to elegant front entrances. A house with a terra-cotta roof has two Jaguars in the drive, one ivory and the other the colour of café-au-lait. What I notice most are details: the copper trim, the glassed-in rooms, the exquisite brick chimneys. This is a neighbourhood that possesses a mature and slouchy richness that only time can bring.

At the end of Elm Avenue is hidden Craigleigh Gardens, almond-shaped and peaceful. Into the gardens a Philippino nanny pushes a stroller with a little blond child in it, followed by a boy on a tricycle and two aging black Labradors. The nanny lifts the child out of the stroller. The boy aims his pistol at a squirrel and gets off three sputtering shots. The dogs, in stately parallel rhythm, move across the park.

MARK DUBOIS sits in his office, his bland and youthful face staring impassively at me. I had never expected to be intimidated by a car salesman, but Mark Dubois, sales manager of Jaguar on Bay, is a block of ice. Why shouldn't he be? The chair I'm sitting in is usually reserved for people whose decision of the week is whether to buy a Porsche, Mercedes, or Jaguar. Mr. Dubois has been as hard to make an appointment with as any CEO.

Behind us in the showroom, the Sovereigns, the XJ6s, the Vandans, and the Coupés are as silent as cats, their beautiful forms shining in the evening light. Yes, Mr. Dubois sighs, Toronto's new wealth has contributed to the increase of sales— seven hundred Jags a year from this one dealership. I make a quick calculation of seven hundred times seventy-thousand dollars, the price of the average Jag. That makes forty-nine million dollars a year.

What do Jag owners have in common? "Wealth," Mr. Dubois says, looking at me as if I am stupid. "Jaguar buyers are wealthy people. There are different ways to become wealthy. Some work for it, others inherit their money. Some of them are very snobbish, but others are nice and genuine. It's a statement, there's no question about it. A Jaguar is a status symbol. It separates itself in the look and the way it drives. I'd say the best word to describe Jaguar is elegance. It's a head-turner, there's no doubt about that. A mid-range BMW is ten thousand dollars less than a Jaguar. Some buyers come in and agonize over whether they should spend the money and make the big leap."

The big leap, the leap of faith. I ask Mr. Dubois if selling Jaguars is different from selling Fords. "The difference is that at this level of clientele you have to understand people better. These are less forgiving buyers. Many of them know each other. They do business together, they belong to the same clubs, they socialize together. Negative feedback travels very quickly."

I thank Mr. Dubois for his time and he gives the barest of nods, unsmiling. Smiles are reserved for buyers.

TOULA SOTIRAKOS takes me through the labyrinthine halls of Orenstein and Partners in the Atrium building and into her own office. On her desk sits a coffee mug emblazoned with the words *Real Women Delegate*.

Toula's dark curls fall over the enormous padded shoulders of her blazer. Three years ago she merged her own accountancy practice with Orenstein and Partners, and it was here that she came up with the idea of the Business Women's Network. The width of her desk is intimidating, and her attitude is serious, yet she is warmer and less suspicious than most of the men I've spoken to. As an immigrant's daughter, she had to work hard to make good, defeating the prejudices against women and outsiders. "In 1960, my dad wouldn't even think of speaking Greek to me on the bus," she says, and I am reminded of how the police chief of Toronto banned meetings in foreign languages in 1929 to prevent workers from organizing.

But Toula is thinking of something else. "Sometimes the immigrants

of this country try to keep their values intact. We try to stay Greek."
After she finished high school, Toula's father said to her: Well, Toula,
are you going to go on to university or are you going to get married?
When Toula did become a CA she didn't take a corporate job where
the hours are more regular as most women accountants do; instead,
her ambitions sent her first to Deloitte Haskins and Sells and then
out on her own. She started the classic ethnic practice: an office
at Danforth and Pape, a tax column for the local Greek newspaper,
a high profile at all the Greek community functions.

But Toula tells me that she wasn't satisfied to be just an ethnic
professional. She started attending the various women's networks
that meet at the Mövenpick and the Inn on the Park. And then she
joined Orenstein and Partners, founded sixty years ago when most
Toronto firms wouldn't hire Jews. But at Orenstein Toula began to
feel that the women's networks were too small-time. So she pitched
a new idea to the partners: a network for women who are already
successful, women who work long hours, make very good money,
and have full-time help bringing up the kids. Even these women,
Toula argued, didn't understand the values of networking. Men start
making their contacts in private school, at university, through their
clubs and golf games. "In business it's not how much you know,
it's who you know," Toula says. "Women don't know where to start.
They're somewhat shy. They don't understand that this is how the
business world operates."

The partners said yes and the network took off. Now it has eight
hundred members and over fifty at a time attend the monthly
breakfast meetings at the Elm Club. While listening to tax specialists
and karate instructors, they get to know one another, trade cards,
open up possibilities. Toula tells of one member who owns her own
construction company and was having a disagreement with her bank.
At the network she sat next to a female bank executive and the two
got along swimmingly. So the woman pulled her accounts from the
old bank and took her business to the new one.

Toula speaks with some pride of her accomplishments, and it's
easy to feel her sense of cause— a feminist cause, even if it also has
the effect of bringing her the right "calibre of clients." Yet Toula has
no interest in bringing feminist values to business, wanting only

to compensate for the backgrounds that women like herself lack. She even expects that the network will become redundant in a few years when women have learned to compete equally with men.

I ask Toula to give a profile of the network's members. "It's basically white and European," she says. "Most have at least one degree or are part of a profession. There really aren't any new ethnics, most of the women went to school here. But there are Greeks, Italians, and a lot of Jewish women. They're really not women who need to look at the social issues like rape. We're not a social or community group. Just as we wouldn't bring in topics like AIDS, or cruelty to animals in cosmetics testing. We don't think that this group would be interested in those sorts of topics."

Toula reaches back into her cabinet to fetch a copy of the women's business directory, leaning next to Jane Fonda's *Women Coming of Age*. I ask her about Toronto's problems, such as the growing number of homeless. "I don't want to sound insensitive," she says, "but for me right now, I don't see this impact. I don't live downtown and see people wheeling shopping carts with their posessions around." She does agree, however, that the traffic is getting worse.

"Look at that," Toula smiles as I get up to leave. "Here I am talking about networking and I almost forgot to give you my card."

SEVERAL LARGE SHEETS have been pinned up to the wall, and on them are written names, most of them male, with a date next to each. The dates go back three and four years, but some are just months ago. "Whenever I sing this song I think of Jan and the energy he had," says the young man in the white blouse. Strumming his acoustic guitar he begins to sing—

Sometimes it seems every moment is a test,
nothing in the outside world can put your mind at rest—

The room in Oakham House on Gould Street is small and cozy, and the man singing stands before a fireplace. The people sitting in the rows of chairs are dressed in running shoes and shorts, and each has a small fabric rainbow pinned to his or her shirt. Listening, their faces do not show shock or disbelief, but a deeper grief and resignation; some are even smiling. After the song, the man puts down his guitar and takes up a candle, white and elegant. "I light this candle in memory of Sam and Mary." Then he touches the flame to the candle held by a man sitting in the first row of chairs. As the first man places his own candle in a small box filled with sand, the second man says, "I light this in memory of Ed." He then lights the candle of the woman beside him.

"I light this in memory of Russel."

"I light this in memory of Greg."

"I light this in memory of all those we have lost," says a man with a neat dark beard and a stud in one ear. His eyes close and shimmer. "There are so many... "

ON THE CUPOLA before Queen's Park a skit is in progress that is genuinely funny. Two people pretending to be tourists from a town called Dullsville are walking down Yonge Street. The sight of the big city fills them with terror. "Oh my God, blue hair!" cries the woman. "A used condom!" gasps the man. A third actor approaches them and says politely, "Excuse me, can you spare some change?" "Ahh!" the couple screams and mimes running away. "We're being swarmed by a youth gang!"

Carmel Hili, the CRC worker who pushed and cajoled to make this "popular culture festival" happen, is carrying packs of juice bottles from the trunk of his car to the food table. Most of the food is free to anyone who asks: apples and bananas, sandwiches, and a sticky-looking vegetarian dish. The preparation that has gone into the festival is obvious— the rented sound equipment, the banners hanging from the cupola, the booth where children can get their faces painted. All that's missing is a crowd, but the afternoon is early yet.

Parika is sitting on one of the benches and I go to join her. Of all the projects that the Bread Not Circuses Coalition is fighting against, the one that I have the most mixed feelings about is the ballet/opera house. And this paralyzing of judgement reminds me of what Oscar Wilde wrote: "The man who sees both sides of the question is the man who sees nothing at all." The supporters have been trying for a new house for a decade, and it's true that the O'Keefe

Centre, where the ballet and opera now perform, is an awful barn. And despite what the coalition likes to say, opera and ballet are not simply elite pleasures enjoyed by the rich. True, on opening nights limousines line up before the O'Keefe, and only the well-heeled can afford to attend the black-tie fundraising balls. But working people, immigrants, and students, too, love the opera and ballet.

On the other side, two hundred and thirty million dollars is an unconscionable amount to spend on just two arts companies when there isn't enough for affordable housing. Opera will still go on at the O'Keefe, but people cannot live without a roof over their heads. How terrible it would be to step out of a new theatre, a great work of public architecture, and over the sleeping body of a homeless person. If it is a matter of one or the other, then surely the answer is easy. Or can we afford such monumental works and still have a just city? Would a new ballet/opera house make these arts more or less accessible to people? On these questions there has been no public discussion, for the Ballet Opera House Corporation has worked largely in secrecy, quietly lobbying politicians and hoping that people will rest passively while it acts on their behalf.

The mood of the festival is upbeat, but the most obvious impression is that there still aren't a lot of people here. Less than a hundred and fifty milling before the cupola, some of whom are organizers and performers, and others mere passersby who have stopped to watch. At one of the booths, two or three people are using plans of the Bay-Wellesley site to draw their own alternatives to the ballet/opera house. The booth has been prepared by Canadian Architects, Designers, and Planners for Social Responsibility— a rather grand name for a group without any formal membership, formed by a couple of young graduate architects named Richard Milgrom and Archie Hughes.

When I met with them recently at a California-style restaurant called Charmers, they came from their offices where Archie was designing condominiums in Pickering and Richard a "monster home" near York Mills Road. Both would have preferred to be working on cooperative housing. Richard complained that some clients were without the "personality" to make their houses interesting; all they wanted were big rooms and monuments to conspicuous consumption. But Richard and Archie have little choice in the work they are assigned. Contrary to their naive expectations as students, architecture is a service industry where integrity means doing a good job on projects one doesn't believe in.

To do the work that drew them to architecture in the first place, Richard and Archie have had to go outside their professional duties. Both are on the board of a non-profit housing group that has renovated five houses between the Don River and the Beach, turning them into cooperatives. But the process is long and tedious, and the funding scarce. "I went into architecture with the idea of making the world a better place," Richard said with an ironic grin. "I seem to have been wrong."

As the next band sets up on the cupola, children run back and forth and activist friends exchange greetings. On the cupola the band begins a song about preventing AIDS adapted from a Paul Simon tune and called "Fifty Ways to Use Your Rubber." Some of the lyrics are making the CBC cameraman laugh but he doesn't roll his camera. The lead singer of the group, a square-set young woman with punk-black hair and an intricate tattoo of a chameleon on her shoulder, has a voice so deep and clear that it mesmerizes the listeners.

Standing on the grass below the cupola is a teenaged boy, thin as a rake, with a bandana tied over his hair. What brings him to my attention is his red T-shirt with an encircled "A" scrawled on it, the symbol of anarchism. Just this morning on the subway I had seen a teenaged girl with that same symbol drawn on her knapsack, reading the colour comics. On billboards, the sides of buildings, the anarchist "A" can be seen spraypainted throughout the downtown, and I have wondered about this supposed revival of anarchist belief. In June of 1988 anarchists from Canada, the United States, and Europe gathered in Toronto and I went to a workshop they held at the 519 Church Community Centre. The anarchists were a mixed and ragged lot, some thoughtful activists, others mere freeloaders. Behind the tables of anarchist literature one man sat naked as he sold his publications. Upstairs, the workshops got bogged down in the same arguments that anarchists were having eighty years ago, only the subject was Nicaragua rather than the Soviet Union.

The freeloaders were probably responsible for the ridiculous scuffle with the police during the final street demonstration, but the television coverage confirmed in most people's minds that all anarchists are violent troublemakers. But I had long admired, if somewhat romantically, the anarchist ideas of individual responsibility and the innate existence of justice, and watching the teenager in the red T-shirt, I wonder whether he knows that Emma Goldman died in Toronto in 1940, and that her body lay in state in the Labour Lyceum on Spadina Avenue. I go up to him and ask about the T-shirt. "No, it isn't what you think," he says quickly. "Somebody gave it to me." He's a Catholic high-school student and was just wandering by. Up close, I can see that the T-shirt is not homemade but mass produced, as if the circled "A" were just another product identification. "At school," he says, "kids have everything they want, so they don't think about people who don't." He listens for a moment to the speaker at the microphone. "They have some good things to say up there."

ON THE PHONE Jennifer told me to meet her at a café on the southwest corner of Winchester and Parliament. But on arriving I wonder if I have made a mistake, for the Old Cabbagetown Delicatessen, with its pretty red-checked table-cloths and gourmet offerings is so unlike the dismal diners where people in the east end usually ask to meet. I buy a peach juice and wait at one of the tables, looking out the window at the day, so warm and close that it's impossible to tell whether the dampness is from humidity or rain. Near me a young woman dressed in black is speaking. "I've always been a person of strong moral values. Like stealing. I'd never do it. Because it's stupid and wrong... "

Hearing my name, I look up to see an out-of-breath woman with wet hair, fine dark features, and brown eyes. "Sorry, I'm late, but my sitter didn't show up. I had to get another, but she's only a kid so I can't stay long."

Jennifer sits down and, speaking rapidly, tells me how her father worked with John Sewell back in the early seventies to stop St. James Town from spreading south of Wellesley Street. Although they were finally successful, the high rises north of Wellesley irrevocably damaged the friendliness and cohesion of the neighbourhood.

Jennifer herself was born in England to a British father and a Jamaican mother, but her parents separated and Jennifer was brought up by her mother. That, she says, is where her concern for poor families comes from and why she is now involved in a political lobby called Wedge, a project to build a home for battered women, a program to encourage inner-city gardens and co-ops, and most especially the group she helped found, Low Income Families Together— LIFT.

Jennifer rhymes off all the neighbourhoods she has lived in— the Danforth, High Park, even Avenue Road and Bloor "before it was yuppified." "Of all the neighbourhoods, the Portuguese were the most racist," she says. "I hate to generalize, but that's the way it was. They'd rent a place to me because they couldn't tell, but my husband was black and when they'd see him they'd start harassing us. Our tires were slashed. Well, maybe it's my historical awareness of what the Portuguese did in Africa," she laughs.

As we speak, Jennifer's sense of history and her identification with the black side of her heritage assert themselves often. In one of the LIFT newsletters that Jennifer has produced, there is a historical review of support for single parents that goes back to 1920, when only widows and the wives of the insane were eligible. Jennifer uses history as support and as weapon. She tells me that her mother was an artist and her father is presently a department head at the University of Toronto, so she had plenty of stimulation as a child. As part of an experiment for bright children when she was at Castle Frank High School, Jennifer went every Saturday morning to special classes and studied university-level subjects such as zoology. "They treated us with respect and dignity," Jennifer says. "It was great. But then we'd go back on Monday to Castle Frank and think, what is this bullshit? I don't know a single kid from Saturday Morning School who didn't drop out of high school. They spoiled it for us."

An only child herself, Jennifer decided early that she wanted to have four children. And she did, the first in 1982 when she was twenty-one, the second in '84, the third in '85, and the baby in '88. Not long after the last she separated from her husband. "In this day and age, in this city, it's a liability to have children. Both parents have to work which I don't think is good for very young kids. My mother was a single mother and I was put in daycare and I hated it and hated her. A lot of feminists don't like me for saying that, but that was my experience. I have made a conscious choice to stay home with my children and so I've chosen poverty. I don't think our society values children. If we did we'd always have funds for kids, we'd have time-share jobs for mothers, we'd build apartments with courtyards so that kids were safe inside. As a child I learned a lot going to the symphony, to plays, you name it. But I can't do that with mine. I'd like to take them to Kiddyland in Ontario Place. But by the time you come home you've spent your week's budget."

Jennifer leans her elbows on the table and talks about the material desires that children pick up and that make being a mother harder. "The struggle between what one is expected to have and what one can have or wants to have puts a lot of pressure on the family. I mean, when I see wealthy people I don't just hate them like some people. Maybe because I'm from a middle-class background myself I know they can be decent human beings. But when I see a kid in super-expensive clothes it does get me upset. I buy new clothes for my kids once a year and the rest of the time it's Goodwill. Shopping at Goodwill, you have to go through all the boxes of clothes and you can't find what you want. It's tiring and frustrating. My kids go to Winchester School. There are kids from St. James Town there— single mothers— from Cityhome— lower class families— and from Cabbagetown— middle and upper-middle class. The other day they had a party at a classmate's. He has a big, beautiful house with a pool in the backyard. It's hard to explain why we can't buy one too. But I've ingrained in them that we're a happy, loving family. I don't think it's so terrible being poor. At least we're not taking advantage of anyone."

I ask Jennifer whether she feels different from the people around her, having come from the middle class, and she nods. "I do feel different. I'm a lot more aware of why they are where they are. And I'm also more understanding. A lot of poor people are very conservative. And they think they've just fucked up, that everything is their fault. I tell them, no, you're an example of what the system does. My work with LIFT is trying to educate people, to help them take control of their lives by creating alternative economies like food co-ops and clothing exchanges. It's really difficult. People feel like outcasts and that they can't make any difference. You can see it where they live— they've got dirty walls, dirty sheets, dirty sofas. They've just given up."

Jennifer remembers that her babysitter has to leave and we get up and walk in the drizzle to her home, she rolling her bike as we cross Prospect Avenue to Rose. The apartment is in a short housing row and Jennifer lets us in. "It took me three years to struggle my way out of a two-bedroom apartment. When my first was born I put my name on the list for Cityhome. Cityhome is an example of a good thing gone wrong. When it first started we thought it was great, the way it fixed up people's apartments. But then it became a big hostile bureaucracy. Josh, did you wake the baby?"

"Yes," comes a small voice from upstairs. And Josh, the second youngest, walks naked into the kitchen. Jennifer calls her apartment a "subsidized mansion," and it's easy to see why as the small rooms are spread on three levels. Still, the apartment feels like a cramped, if happy, mess, with pillows and newspapers, children's drawings and clothing everywhere. Jennifer fishes a pair of underwear from the portable dryer and pulls them onto Josh just as her other sitter comes in, a big teenaged girl with a shaved head. The sitter picks up the woken baby and, coming back into the kitchen, hands her to Jennifer as the telephone rings. Just then the two oldest children come in, eating Mr. Freezes and full of the story of how they won them at the playground. "The Grand Central Station disease," Jennifer rolls her eyes and returns to her telephone argument with one of the LIFT members, all the while holding the baby and stuffing the portable washer with clothes.

The sitter gets the kids to play in the den so that Jennifer and I can sit in the kitchen over a cup of tea. The phone call has exasperated her, for she and her partner who founded LIFT are already disagreeing over the organization's structure. The more radical partner doesn't want LIFT to turn into a bureaucracy like those they're criticizing, but Jennifer thinks that a businesslike approach is still necessary once they open the resource centre and hire staff. Yet Jennifer understands her concern. "A lot of things start with really good intentions and then fuck up. They start playing the game and then the professionals who can stomach it come in and take over. Pretty soon the poor people drift away."

Jennifer describes the resource centre as a place where low income families will meet to help each other, but she's most excited about the videos LIFT wants to make. Because of innumeracy— the difficulty of understanding numbers— the poor don't know just what society is up to. Eight percent of the population controls fifty percent of the wealth, she says, but what does that really mean and look like? As an example, Jennifer compares the numbers one million and one billion. When the government is going to spend a billion, or somebody makes a billion, what does that mean? Well, she says, a million seconds would take eleven days to pass. A billion seconds would take thirty-two years. That's what a billion dollars is.

Lorris, the oldest boy, wants to go outside. "But it's pouring rain," Jennifer coos.

"It ain't pouring," says Lorris.

"How about doing some homework? Or making me another nice sunset like the one we put on the fridge? Do you want to build a highway for your brother? I don't think anything I suggest is going to be satisfactory, is it?"

The daughter wanders in and Jennifer gets her a drink before sitting down again. "Downtown in City Hall there's a lot of slimy two-faced politics. They set up a community development fund— Lorris, don't do that!— and then made it so difficult to get at that the fund never really got used. And the program Healthiest Babies Possible was like that too. I went when I was last pregnant to get milk vouchers and they told me that I could have them only if I took the prenatal classes. Look, I said, I've had three kids already, I think I know what I'm doing, I've even got a midwife. But my kids need milk. They still wouldn't give me the vouchers and I never got them. The bureaucrats don't ask the clients what they need and they never follow up with studies to see if the programs are effective. They'll schedule a training class for eight thirty in the morning when people can't get there because they have to get their kids to school. Then when no one shows up they say the classes aren't needed. Or look at the community centres that they spend millions of dollars building. All they're used for is craft classes and the gym. There are women suffering from isolation and starvation and they teach them how to build things with popsicle sticks."

Jennifer's own family benefits have just been raised to nine hundred and eighty-five dollars a month but she hasn't yet told Cityhome, which adjusts her rent to one-quarter of her income. "Well, the Cityhome form came two days before I found out about the increase and so I just put the old figure down," she laughs. "But it's the system. They make you cheat to survive. I know the rest of the public looks down on single mothers on assistance and calls us lazy bums. But more than half is spent on administration. It's a waste of money. We at the lower end are always trying to confine ourselves into categories that they will accept. We're treated as types, not human beings. Middle class social workers have a real attitude. They don't understand the exhaustion of being poor. To go to a food bank I have to get a baby sitter and take the subway. Then I suffer through the attitude of having fucked up. Then I look at the food and don't even want it. I'm fussy and I'm very sensitive to additives. You feel humiliated, like shit. And every time you're in a position to need help they have an opportunity to come into your life."

Jennifer leans back in her chair and talks about one way she makes life easier. Shoplifting. "I steal my cheese and my salmon because they're expensive and small. Usually I have a few screaming kids around me and I just drop something into the stroller. If the cashier doesn't see it I don't say anything. Then I go down the street and with the money I saved buy fresh vegetables and juice. I don't feel guilty about it at all. I would never steal a luxury— if I want something I'll save up for it— and never from a small store or from another person. But the Dominion has a lot of nerve setting up in St. James Town and charging higher prices."

Another way is to take her kids to all the free concerts and events she can. She agrees that most poor don't take advantage of them. "A lot of poor people are too busy trying to survive. They don't know it's even there. When you're low-nourished and oppressed and depressed it's hard to bundle up the kids, pack a lunch, and go there. The poor people who go are either the arts community or the lefties."

As we get up, Jennifer tells me how she hopes to make a paying job for herself out of LIFT and that she doesn't expect to remain poor forever. "I want eventually to earn enough money to be comfortable and take my kids on trips and stuff like that. I don't think that makes me a money-grubbing zealot," she adds defensively. We pass Josh's room, where he is sitting cross-legged and swooshing a space cruiser about. Jennifer suggests that I talk to one of her friends who is a working mother and as I readily agree the two of us go outside, Jennifer to run errands. Glancing back, she smiles and says, "I love to escape."

The Miss Toronto Pageant

THE POLITICIANS hadn't counted on so many people turning up— over two hundred— and after cramming into the stifling cafeteria of Bloor Collegiate, we are instructed to move en masse to the equally stifling auditorium. The school was built in the late twenties and the auditorium is a shell of rising seats with intricate plasterwork on the walls. Down below, the janitors wrestle unsuccessfuly with the microphones, while the diminutive Joe Pantalone, a Metro councillor, tries to make his thin voice carry to the back row.

Richard Gilbert, the other Metro councillor, tells how the push to reduce drug trafficking along Bloor Street between Christie Pits and Ossington Avenue has moved it further west into their neighbourhood. But the man who rivets everyone's attention is Superintendent John Getty of Fourteenth Division, a square-jawed man, elderly and almost brittle-looking, with an Irish brogue like cops in gangster pictures. He tells the pent-up crowd how last night in Ottawa with Mayor Eggleton he told the federal minister of justice that people are afraid to walk the streets, that Toronto is waging a drug war. Two women in the front row turn and nod vigorously at one another. Crack, cocaine, heroine, and marijuana are what's being found at busts by the division's eight-man drug squad. "It's going to be the ruination of our country." While Superintendent Getty does not want to see Canada turn into a police state, he muses that we may have gone too far in protecting individual rights.

Superintendent Getty believes that anyone convicted of a drug offence ought to get a minimum one year sentence. "I'll be honest with you," he chortles, "I enjoy putting people in jail."

A woman in the audience stands up. Why don't the police close down the donut shop at St. Clarens Avenue when everyone knows drug-dealing goes on there? Wild applause. Other places are called out— a restaurant, a pool hall. Superintendent Getty says, "Half our bloody trouble started when we allowed twenty-four hour openings." Claps of approval. Another man gets up— why are people allowed to loiter on the streets? He remembers a time when the cops made you move on. Superintendent Getty offers his theory for the increase in loitering, prostitution, and drugs in Toronto: "We elected a guy named Pierre Elliott Trudeau." A mixture of applause and shouts. "In 1982 he brought in the Charter of Rights," says the superintendent, "and as far as I can see the only people it's benefited are the criminals." Applause, cat-calls— the meeting is getting out of hand. A studious looking black man in a turtleneck and wire glasses gets up. He restrains himself from defending the charter and merely suggests that we stay on the subject at hand. Superintendent Getty diplomatically compliments the man on his point of view.

A woman rises. She called 911 three times while a white Barracuda in front of her house acted as a mobile drugstore. The cops never came. "I see them, three police cars at a restaurant, chitchatting for hours." A small Italian man says, "It's not the police I'm complaining about. They're doing a hell of a fine job. It's the politicians' fault."

A man rises and angrily points at the stage. "My two-year old son brought a needle into the house from the back yard!" He shouts this out several times. A woman nutritionist from the high school says that some teenagers buy their lunches with fifty, even hundred-dollar bills. Several people who speak appear to wish to tell their life stories. A young man of Asian descent talks about his experiences as a social worker. Not long ago he saw a cop making a drug arrest by kicking a teenager in the stomach. The police should be working with the kids, not beating them up. "The cop should have shot him!" someone shouts. Applause, loud calls, arguments. "Make your point, make your point!" Joe Pantalone tries to calm the audience down, reminding us that democracy means people get to speak and be heard. But the meeting has gone past nine o'clock and the janitors want to go home.

"I'm a school trustee," a man in front says, "and you can stay as long as you like."

WALKING BY THE HIGHRISES of St. James Town is a weird and disorienting experience, as if I had suddenly materialized in some housing project in the Bronx. The buildings make my heart plummet, with their bland grass and cement grounds and the concrete awnings scooped brutally over the entrances. This seems like some strange city in the sea of Toronto, an Atlantis that ought to have sunk forever.

Unlike Regent Park, St. James Town was built by private developers who were allowed to tear down the blocks of run down houses and put up Le Corbusier's Garden City of the future. Now people reside here as tenants of the Metro Toronto Housing Authority. And at thirty storeys high, Two-Hundred Wellesley is the biggest of the St. James Town buildings, a real monster. Seven hundred and eleven apartments, twelve hundred tenants. Inside, the lobby is dreary but clean and on the wall is a sign: NO LOITERING OR PLAYING GAMES. The elevator has metal sides to discourage graffiti.

In her nineteenth-floor apartment, Vickie Rennie lies on the flowery sofa like Cleopatra accepting submissions from her subjects. She is a small woman with a face round as a balloon, dyed blond hair and black eyebrows. Vickie suffers from severe arthritis and has had her knees and feet rebuilt several times. She supplements her disability pension by selling Avon. The two-bedroom apartment Vickie shares with her mother has orange carpeting wall-to-wall, a display of collector spoons on the arch before the horseshoe kitchen, and a huge television in a colonial-style cabinet. Above Vickie hangs a fluorescent painting of the Toronto skyline. The coffee table before her is covered with bottles of over the counter painkillers and prescription capsules.

Vickie and her mother moved in nineteen years ago when the building was spanking new. "Nobody lives in an MTHA building because they want to," Vickie says, yet she and her mother are proud of the home they've made together. It's because of their pride that when Two-Hundred Wellesley became a virtual war zone they decided to take it back. Now Vickie is a local celebrity. She has spoken on Metro Morning and made the front page of the *Star*.

"By 1986, this place was hell town," Vickie says, lighting up a cigarette. She describes how the dealers first began to move in, one or two at first, offering free crack to the tenants to get them hooked. One dealer befriended a vulnerable woman who lived alone, moved in with her, and turned her place into a crack house. Tenants who got hooked would start to steal or take up prostitution to feed their addictions. Vickie describes a crack house: an apartment with no furniture, just roaches and mice; twenty or more people lying about stoned among the mounds of matches, spoons, and freebasing equipment; blood splattered on the walls from "red-flagging"— drawing out blood with a syringe to mix with the crack before injecting it again.

Two-Hundred Wellesley became a no-man's land, Vickie says. Old and disabled people wouldn't leave their apartments for fear of being mugged in the corridors. Tenants found needles in elevators, used condoms tossed onto their balconies from the apartments above. Hookers turned tricks on the front lawn and underneath the stairwells. One evening her mother entered the lobby and saw a pimp holding a knife to a woman's throat while he accused her of holding out money. Vickie saw a man crash his head through the glass wall of the balcony above. One night a body with its throat slit was dumped in the lobby.

Vickie had never been politically involved before, but when finally she had had enough she decided to organize the kind of Neighbourhood Watch program that exists on streets with houses. The first meeting was a failure; people were too terrified of the dealers to join. But then the arrests started. After weeks of difficult surveillance, the police began kicking down doors. For days the task-force van was parked in front and when the police came out with a dealer in handcuffs the people on the benches outside would cheer. In a month the police shut down ten crack houses.

When Vickie tried to organize again the residents felt secure enough to help her form Vertical Watch. Vickie worried about her own safety, but the worst that ever happened was the bag of human excrement left on her doorstep. Now every second floor has a "captain" who keeps an eye on things and reports daily to Vickie. "It's gotten so good that 51 Division doesn't keep a file on us anymore." Tenants started to speak to one another in the elevator and Two-Hundred Wellesley has become a good place to live again.

To celebrate, Vickie came up with the idea of an open house. The police and the security company with whom she had closely worked were supportive and small companies donated food and prizes for the kids. The large corporations were another story. McDonalds gave free cups but made Vertical Watch pay for the orange drink. Giant Weston Bakeries told Vickie that if it decided her cause was worthy enough it would allow her to buy its hot dog buns for thirty-five percent off.

But the open house was a big hit, and over five hundred people celebrated the born-again building. "The morale is even better than when we first moved in," Vickie says. "The kids are playing outside again. I haven't seen a used condom in God knows how long." While she points out the roles that the police, MTHA, and the security company played in saving the building, it could not have happened without her own doggedness. And although she doesn't say it, Vickie is worried about what will happen to Vertical Watch when she wants to step down. Who will make the daily contacts with the captains and keep up the enthusiasm?

"I read something in the paper that made me so irate," she says. "A woman was blasting MTHA because her father fell in his apartment and broke his hip and nobody found him for over two days. She wants somebody from MTHA to check on the old tenants every day. Well, what about her, for bloody's sake? She's his daughter. People expect too much."

Vickie rises from the sofa and takes me to the balcony to show off the view. She points down to what at first looks like a vacant lot but is actually the foundation of a building that was abandoned when the developer went bankrupt. One day smoke appeared from the underground garage entrance and when the police went down below they found mattresses and sofas. People were living there. "That's how desperate they are," she says.

Still, Vickie can lean on the rusted balcony rail and sigh with contentment. What one sees from here most of all is a green canopy of trees softening the city. "You could live in this area and never leave it," she says. "People say it's getting like New York. But I look out from this balcony and think, not yet."

SOUTH OF ST. JAMES TOWN, on Queen Street East, is a big and disorderly used bookstore in an row of old commercial storefronts. Upstairs in the office, Ascher Joram, the proprietor of Acadia Book Store, conducts the real business of buying and selling art books among a network of collectors and dealers. Many of the city's other book dealers are on fashionable Queen Street West, if they can still afford the rent, but Ascher has been here for twenty years, though he and his wife now live in Don Mills. One might say that Ascher has lived three lives: first, as a Jew in Germany; then in Palestine before it became Israel; and finally Canada. Not long ago I'd heard two of Ascher's companions in the book trade groaning over their friend's refusal to leave the east end. Misplaced loyalty, they called it.

And so I've come to find out why Ascher has stayed. But I was mistaken in assuming he would sing the praises of the east end and defend it from its detractors. Ascher speaks with a German accent, sprinkles his talk with Yiddish, and suffers from high blood pressure. Over his cluttered desk he unfolds a map of Toronto. On it he has drawn a small square two inches high, enclosing the area around his store. "Do you know how much assisted housing there is in this neighbourhood?" he asks. "How many hostels? How many homes for psychiatric patients? Hmmm?"

Ascher's angry tone startles me, but in a moment I realize he doesn't expect an answer. This is the most densely subsidized neighbourhood in the country and still the projects go up. "Try to find out what's happening," he says bitterly. "You need a full-time job! Know what the title of your book should be? *The Creation of the Biggest Slum in the Country.*"

The municipal and provincial governments, Ascher believes, are destroying the east end by putting here the poor, alcoholic, and mentally ill, turning it into the "dumping ground of the city." Not only is this a disaster for the businesses in the neighbourhood and the homeowners whose property is decreasing in value, but it is also a disaster for the poor. How can it be healthy, Ascher asks, to put poor single mothers and their children in a neighbourhood rife with drug dealers? Why not put them in the suburbs, or even somewhere like Barrie, where the influences are more benign? The simple reason, Ascher nods vehemently, is that those neighbourhoods have the political clout to keep the undesirables out.

I say that government philosophy these days calls for mixed-income neighbourhoods, not concentrations of rich and poor. Ascher snorts. "Don't listen to what they say. See what they're doing. I've been involved for years with this lousy city hall. The politicians are a bunch of hypocrites. And the more they pretend to be socialists the worse they are. Morally, they're totally corrupt. We understand it's not Forest Hill here, but why treat people as third-class citizens? Tell me, why is it permitted for people to shit and piss on your door while if that happened in Rosedale the police would be there in two minutes? What's illegal everywhere else is all right here. The Royal Bank closed its branch here after seventy years. Claimed it was losing money, but the Royal just had its most profitable quarter ever. They saw what was happening here. Now I hear the T-D Bank would like to get out too. They're the only branch that is paid to cash government cheques without identification. You know why? Because they don't want the people on welfare coming up to Bay Street. They want to keep them down here."

From a bulging file on his desk, Ascher pulls out some papers. He shows me the architectural plans that have turned his anger into a final raging despair. In the Moss Park housing project to the east, Metro Toronto Housing Authority is going to fill the open spaces between the highrises with low-level housing units. The plan is meant to alleviate some of the project's vandalism and drugselling, but Ascher is convinced that more low-income housing will be catastrophic. "I've talked to the police and they can't control the crime in these highrises. And the government wants to build more housing there? Can you imagine the chutzpah? They'll have to go in with machine guns!"

Ascher is becoming so agitated that I worry about his blood pressure. "Just try and fight it," he says. "They will portray you as being the rich against the poor and homeless. But it's the people of this area who have supported those in need more than anybody else. Do you ever see the politicians coming down here?" He takes from his file a snapshot of a dishevelled man with a beard like Walt Whitman, leaning on the Acadia Books storefront. "This guy lived in my doorway for fifteen years. How much do you think he cost me? Never mind the lost business, I mean the two or three dollars I gave him every day for ten years. Could I let him starve? One night he finally froze to death. But most of these people on the street here are not the harmless alcoholics like the old days. In front of my store I see brutal fights. In the restaurants they do their drug deals shamelessly in the open. I'm not like these bleeding hearts— I wouldn't give these guys hanging out on the streets one nickel. Why won't they work? What do they want to be, head of General Motors? Where is the pride in people?"

Ascher shakes his head. "Where will it end? The system's going to collapse."

THIS IS THE THIRD time in two weeks that I witness a beggar being removed from a restaurant. The restaurant today is the Toby's at the Eaton Centre, the beggar is big and shaggy, and the waiter who removes him is an earringed young black man. The waiter is uncomfortable in his role and the shaggy man doesn't want to leave; meanwhile, we diners prefer not to see what is going on. As he is ushered out, the shaggy man half-turns and puts his fist against the waiter's side— but gently. A symbolic punch.

Eaton's has come far since Timothy opened his first drygoods store in 1869 at the corner of Yonge and Queen. Almost twenty years ago the company began assembling the land for the Eaton Centre, secretly planning the development that would re-make fifteen acres of downtown. Now the Eaton Centre claims itself as the heart of the city, and its advertisements glow with the sophistication of an idealized urban life. But in reality it is an oversized mall with the same national chains as malls everywhere and the same pretend-streets lined with potted trees.

Leaving Toby's, I walk down the crowded "street" towards the Dundas atrium. Before the entrance to Eaton's is a space where musicians perform occasionally for the pleasure of passing shoppers, and it was here that the Purple People Eaters, a group of young Toronto artists, performed during Toronto Arts Week. Their work played on the Eaton Centre's promotion as the heart of the city. To the sound of Indian music, an actor dressed as a surgeon bent over a female patient. When he cut into her blouse with a scissors, the woman screamed as artificial blood spurted about. The surgeon removed her heart (actually a ball of dough) and fried it in a large wok. Some of the audience stared uncomprehendingly, some frowned, others laughed. The Eaton Centre was not amused; security guards interfered with the performance and, after it was over, removed the performers from the mall.

I pass through the aisles in Eaton's and out the glass entrance to the street. Neither Eaton's nor the developer, Fairview, had intended the entrance to become a gathering place for possessed evangelists and kids in Guns N' Roses T-shirts. Still, this crowd is, for better or worse, the Eaton Centre's only genuine character trait.

I have come here hoping to talk to some street kids, but the kids hang around in packs, making them hard to approach. Glancing at a newspaper, I lean against the outside doors next to three teenaged boys with shaved heads and wearing Doc Martens. One of the girls with them is dressed alike, with a rat tail hanging at the back of her shaved scalp; but the other looks different, with her neat blond bangs, big preppy jacket and stonewashed jeans, like a girl from the suburbs. The girl with the rat tail is bouncing from foot to foot with crazy energy and talking fast. "This guy was chasing me around with his fucking dick hanging out of his pants. It was this big!" She shows three inches with her fingers. "I told him to fuck off and he called me a fourteen-year-old bitch. When I'm seventeen! You ever fucked a guy with a small dick? It's gross, man, you think it's only half way in."

The boy in a torn leather jacket says, "Are you telling me that you're a Satanic Skinhead? I've been a skinhead for seven years and I've never heard of them. And I've been to Vancouver and everything. So what are you saying, that you have to do time to be one? That's no big deal."

Another boy with a beard sprouting from a youthful chin says, "Who are you most afraid of, a big guy or a psycho? Sure it helps to be big, but if a guy can't fight? It's the little ones you got to be afraid of. A guy with a gun, all he can do is blow you away. But a guy who'll open your stomach and take out your entrails— "

"Like Riff?" the third boy says. "He cut off that guy's ear and sent it to his mother."

Their voices lower as they talk about somebody being shot and thrown off a bridge. Are they telling the truth or bluffing? Their voices are a mixture of bravado and uncertainty. One of them turns his head and gives me a hard stare. I bury my face in the newspaper.

VICKI PENNICK, the head nurse of Covenant House, is telling me of the seventeen-year-old alcoholic boy who had come in from the streets. As he sat miserably on the examination table she asked him if he wanted a motherly hug and, putting out his arms to her, he cried his eyes out. On his second visit the boy asked Vicki for a date. "These kids have undeveloped social skills," she says. "They can't differentiate kinds of relationships."

I have already taken a tour of Covenant House's two buildings on Gerrard Street, the intake centre and the residence. When the house opened in 1982 as a shelter for street kids, it had thirty beds, but now eighty or more sleep here every night, and those who can't get rooms make do with mattresses on the floor. When I took my tour, some of the new arrivals who weren't yet on a school or work-training program were flaked out on mattresses or sprawled on sofas, filling in those bewildering holes of sleep deprivation.

Even when Covenant House increases its number of beds, it will hardly touch the number of kids living on Toronto's streets. Five thousand? Ten? Nobody knows for sure, only that they come from across Ontario, from out west, from the Maritimes. Sometimes a big city's problems aren't all of its own making; like a scapegoat, it takes on the sins and wounds of the country.

Vicki Pennick is an enthusiastic woman with a pleasantly exaggerated emotional manner. Every day she sees the simple consequences of dirt, sleeplessness, malnutrition, and long periods of tension: low-level viruses, upper-respiratory illnesses, gastro-intestinal ailments, wounds, sexually-transmitted diseases, mysterious rashes. Vicki seems to have the most natural rapport with boys, and she talks amusedly of their desperate flirtations and need for motherly affection. "The biggest guys are such babies. I tell my kids, they can speak to me about anything." She tells how a boy who came in last night recounted to her wide-eyed nurses his experiences as a prostitute. Vicki herself is almost strangely upbeat, as if she were protected by a professional and good-natured detachment. But at least Vicki is here; for she confirms what I had heard from a nurse at Neighbourhood Information Post— that most doctors refuse to provide medical attention to homeless people, disliking their presence in the waiting room and their erratic behavior.

When I ask Vicki about the girls she becomes more serious. "The girls are more damaged," she nods. "Guys will leave home if their parents are too strict. One more yelling and they're out of there, they're history. They think it's cool and Yonge Street is glamorous. But girls don't leave home unless it's serious. They're taught to take more without complaining. And once they're on the street they get more abuse. When they come here they're much more suspicious and harder to break down."

Leaving Covenant House, I stand on Gerrard Street and feel my frustration at not talking to the street kids themselves; after all, it's much easier to speak to a professional like Vicki Pennick. While sometimes I have felt that the poor were almost shamefully easy to see, I have just as often felt that the real Toronto, the city living beneath the surface, was eluding me. This sense of defeat brings to mind terms used since the nineteenth century to describe the other side of life, terms like "the secret city" or "hidden poverty." But these terms are false; poverty might be hidden from me, the lives of the homeless might be unknown to me, but they are no secret to those who live them. It is we, not they, who have built the visible and invisible walls that hide them.

So far the only conversation I have had with a kid who has lived on the street was with Julian, a seventeen-year-old who was hunched over the Olympia typewriter in the office of Beat the Street, a literacy program for the homeless. Julian told me that he had been on the street since he was twelve and that even now he was living in hostels, shifting from one to another as his time expired. He was an exotic looking young man, with a rich mane of hair and a languorous tenor's voice. I asked him if the reason he couldn't find a permanent place to live was the lack of money, available apartments, time, or prejudice of his being black or effeminate. "All of them," he drawled. Julian said that he was taking a course in counselling but that it wasn't going well; the day before a drunken client had attacked him, and Julian had needed seven stiches in his side.

"It's very discouraging," he sighed and went back to pecking at the typewriter.

I walk west on Gerrard to the southern edge of Allan Gardens. The gardens were opened in 1860, and the glass and metal Palm House in 1910 to nurture exotic flowers. Street kids often hang out here, having no other place to go. But while I want to meet them, it's hard not to feel nervous. Not long ago I met a man who, strolling through the park at night, was jumped by a gang of kids, robbed and beaten.

On a bench a young man with curling red hair is sitting with his arms outstretched. His thin face needs a shave and on his shoulder is a highly-detailed tattoo of an eagle with its claws extended. His name is Tim and he invites me to sit down. The problem, he says, is that these sixteen-year-old kids ought to be home working at McDonald's rather than peddling dope on Yonge Street. Tim himself is eighteen, which he obviously considers a whole different age, and, although he claims never to have been a street kid, has stayed at Covenant House several times. "I came from Mississauga," he says as if it were on the other side of the Rockies. "I don't have a father and my mother is a cheap slut. I know it's not very nice to say that about your mother but it's the truth. I don't keep in touch with her anymore. But I know she cares and everything. I left home when I was fourteen. Back then I thought that Yonge Street would be glamorous, lined with crowds of people. It isn't glamorous at all. It's just a four-lane street."

Gazing idly toward Gerrard Street, Tim mentions that he just got out of prison. What was he in for? "A whole lot of shit"— mostly for stealing cars. "I never hurt anybody. I stole a lot of cars, though. Nothing older than an '86 and nothing worth under ten thousand. A lot of Reliants. A couple of brand new Vettes. There are four chop shops just around here that buy them for a couple of thousand, strip them down, remake them and sell them again. But I'm through with crime. How was jail? Jail was jail. I was in Maplehurst, out on the 401. They make you work so the time went fast. And you get paid minimum wage. You have to pay board, but even then you save fifty bucks a week. I came out with eleven hundred dollars. The time goes fast except when you're in the hole. It's a four-by-six foot room and they feed you nothing but beancake. Gives you the runs. But I'm through with that stuff because the cops always get you in the end. I've got a job starting tomorrow as a cleaner at the Skydome. The pay is eight ninety-one an hour, pretty good. I'm just going to work and hang out here with my friends and smoke dope. It seems to me that if we're not bothering anybody the cops ought to leave us alone. Pretty soon they'll be calling me and my friends a gang."

Tim waves his arm at a figure crossing the park. The figure approaches and Tim introduces me to Gary, who gives me a brisk handshake. Gary is a short sinewy guy, bow-legged and with hyperactive movements. As he and Tim start to talk I have a hard time following their conversation. Tim mentions a girl named Val whose lights he is going to punch out when he finds her. "You got a smoke, man?" Gary asks. Tim is reluctant to use up his last cigarette. "Light it up, man, light it up." Gary speaks with difficulty and has the look of an overwound toy, ready to burst. He tells of the drugs he took the night before, making a gesture with his arm like stirring a pot or turning a big wheel that leaves me perplexed. But even I understand his miming of an injection into the arm. "Man," Tim shakes his head, "I'm going to stay away from that shit. It'll fuck you up."

The two begin to discuss an incident in which they stood around smiling as a friend gave somebody the boot over and over. And then suddenly Tim and Gary decide to leave, shake my hand, and as they walk away Gary makes that stirring motion again. He calls out, "You ought to know, to us rock is candy. And dope is garr."

"Garr?" I say.

"Garr."

ESCAPE. That's all I can think of, sitting on the Queen Street car as it rattles east over the Don River. Talking to Tim and Gary has depressed me; while they were quite friendly, I would prefer not to meet them at the wrong moment. The streetcar passes through neighbourhoods that are anonymous to those who don't live there. Generations before me have fled to the Beach for a brief respite from the congestion of the city and an illusion of being somewhere else for a short while. Just past the race track I get down, only to be disconcerted by the changes of just the last couple of years. This part of Queen Street too has been infiltrated by the upscale boutique chains, Timothy's and Cultures and Club Monaco, that are scrubbing the streets clean of character.

But south of Queen Street the beach and the boardwalk have not changed. Windsurfers with their brightly-coloured sales glide by as a wave soaks into the sand. Radio sounds are muffled by the breeze that smells of coconut suntan lotion. Young couples billow sheets into the air and settle them down again on the beach while on the boardwalk people wheel baby carriages, mountain bikes, skateboards.

If I try hard enough I can almost see back to when men wore hats and women long skirts as they walked up and down the boardwalk, fanning themselves with their handkerchiefs, talking in Yiddish, Russian, Italian. Towards the east the lake spreads out to the horizon, green-blue and endless. A puppy yelps at a little girl in the shallows. Teenage boys ride the edge of the wave on surfboards shaped like guitar picks. Watching from the wooden benches that face the boardwalk are white-haired women, their hands leaning on their canes.

Halfway down the beach the lifeguard station looks like a lighthouse. By the food kiosk seagulls dive to the waste bins and children line up for ice cream bars and french fries. Even the public washroom, with its echoing concrete walls and faint odour of urine reminds me of childhood excursions to the beach. Beyond here, past the end of the boardwalk, rises the C.R. Harris Water Filtration Plant, that strangely beautiful palace of water. I cannot see it without thinking of Michael Ondaatje's novel, *In the Skin of a Lion*, and the character Patrick Lewis. Patrick, swimming up the intake pipe with a bomb to blow up the plant with its rich arhitectural detail, its herringbone tile in the bathrooms. To blow it up for the workers who laboured and died to build another vulgar monument for the wealthy. But even the fictional Patrick couldn't do it, couldn't destroy this excessive and glorious building.

Two young men stride by me on the sandy planks of the boardwalk. The one in knee-length shorts says, "You should see the beach in Mexico. It's a lot better."

ON THIS HOT DAY oppressed by periodic thunderstorms, I wander disconsolately into the Palm House in Allan Gardens. The Palm House is an exotic miracle of Tasmanian Gum Trees and Brazilian ferns, a moist nurturing of growth beneath arches of painted iron and glass. I walk down the narrow flagstone paths and stare at the pigmy date palms from Vietnam with their long delicate fronds and the wild Strelitzia Nicolai, its tremendous paddle-shaped leaves looming above. Ahead, two teenage girls come out of the ladies room, one with her black hair soaking wet— presumably she has put her head under the tap— and as they go by the one with the wet hair says something to me that I can't pick up.

"Sorry?" I say.

"Nothing, it was just a joke, forget it." She is pale and wild looking, a slim wisp in a white T-shirt with the word VOGUE on it and a pair of tight pocketless jeans. They pass me and go out of the greenhouse. I follow after them.

Outside the Palm House, I follow a garden path and see them again in the open space of the park above Gerrard Street. Beneath a large tree, the curly-haired one lets herself fall onto her stomach and the black-haired girl lets go of her little black purse and leans over to talk to her. Drops of rain are falling from the sky, but under the tree the ground is drier and as I come under its branches I introduce myself awkwardly and ask if I might talk to them.

"No!" says the curly-haired one sprawled on her stomach, her voice muffled because her hand is leaning against her mouth.

"Yes, stay," says the other who is obviously distraught. She paces frenetically back and forth. "I don't know what to do. If anything happens I would never forgive myself. Maybe I should get Dean."

"Don't get Dean," says the muffled voice.

"That's Cheryl," the black-haired girl says, without telling me her own name. "We were drinking vodka all morning, right? But Cheryl's allergic to vodka and I'm afraid something is going to happen to her. But I could never let that happen and now I don't know what to do."

Cheryl just lies there, breathing.

"Do you want me to tell the police over there?" I say. For several police cars hover on Gerrard Street, containing an anti-abortion protest that had been going on all day.

"No, not the cops," the black-haired girl says. "Cheryl, you're sick and it's my fault and if anything happens I don't know what I'd do. If you passed out I wouldn't know what to do— "

"I'm all right," Cheryl mutters.

"How about Covenant House?" I suggest, remembering the nurses.

"No, we can't, we got kicked out of Covenant House. Cheryl's got six months before she can go back and I've got forty-two days. We didn't have any sleep last night. We went to Robertson House and this woman— " she says the word with contempt— "chased us all around, wanting to be our pimp. We had to leave and she chased us all the way to Covenant House and they wouldn't let us in and I was so scared. And now we're ripped on vodka, I had eleven shots, and Cheryl's allergic to vodka and I don't know what to do. I'm going to go get Dean. You stay here and watch her, okay?"

"No, don't go, Darlene," says Cheryl.

"I'll be back in two minutes," Darlene says and she walks quickly but unsteadily down to Gerrard Street.

"Are you all right?" I ask Cheryl. She can't be more than sixteen, a stocky girl lying on her stomach. Various slogans are written in marker on her cut-off jeans, but the only one I can make out is *ALWAYS IN LOVE*.

"Are you all right?"

"Yeah. I don't even know who I'm talking to."

"I'm Cary," I say.

"I can't even see your face," she says without opening her eyes. And then she convulses, not hard, and a little vomit burbles from her mouth onto her hand and arm. She vomits three times, though not much.

"Sit up," I say. "You don't want to choke."

"I can't sit up."

We sit silently for a while. "Darlene's worried about you," I say. "Have you been friends a long time?"

"A long time," Cheryl says. "I can't even go to my mother because she's working."

"You don't live with your mother?"

"Uh-uh," she says. "I had a job and everything before they kicked me out. As a camp counsellor at Harbourfront, five days a week. And I lost it two days ago, after they kicked me out of Covenant House. You can't go to work if you don't have a place to live."

She stops talking and appears to be falling asleep, which worries me.

"Are you falling asleep?" I ask.

"No," she says.

After a while Darlene comes back, alone. "Are you all right, Cheryl?" Cheryl doesn't answer. "We shouldn't have drunk that vodka, it's my fault," Darlene says. She can't keep still and her voice breaks, as if she might cry. She has pale blue eyes, a small nose, and her skin is far too white. "We went to see an apartment this morning, we want to get a place of our own," she explains as she paces. "And the guy gave us vodka. I drank eleven shots. And then he put this porno movie on the VCR and asked if we wanted to see his bedroom— for the decorating," she sneers. "We got out of there. I'm going to go get Dean."

"Darlene, don't."

But she's gone again. This time Cheryl and I don't talk much and she appears to sleep. After a while, Darlene comes across the park with four young men, two with long hair and no shirts. They have tans and young, almost hairless chests.

"Here comes Darlene with some guys," I say.

"Oh no, I can't believe she's doing this. I feel like such a fucking idiot."

They come up. "Hi, Cheryl," one of the guys grins. An amateur tatoo is etched below his rib, spelling out LSD.

"Hello, Dean."

The other guys say hello, too. "I'm so worried about it, she's allergic to vodka," Darlene says.

"She's all right, she's just plastered, that's all."

"Of course I'm all right, Dean. I can recognize your voice, can't I? And aren't my eyes closed? And you too, Scott."

Cheryl has raised her voice considerably. She is obviously all right.

"Let her enjoy the buzz," says Dean. "Just don't roll over onto your back, Cheryl." And the guys troop off together.

"I can't believe you did that to me," Cheryl grins but with her eyes still closed. "That's so embarrassing, for Dean to see me like this. And Scott." She sounds like any teenage girl worried about what the boys will think of her. She might be blushing.

"You should stand up, Cheryl," Darlene insists. "You might choke."

"I can't stand up," Cheryl yells. "Or I'll barf."

"You'll get it out of your system."

"I'm not moving."

"You ought to thank this guy for watching over you. He almost saved your life."

"Hardly," I say.

"I can't even see his face," says Cheryl.

"He's from Evergreen," Darlene says.

"I'm not from Evergreen. I'm a writer, that's all."

"You mean an author? You want to write a book?" Darlene says.

Darlene takes off again, this time to get a cigarette. While she is gone the four young men, with a couple of additions, swing through the park again and stop under our tree. "God, I can't believe you're seeing me like this," Cheryl smiles. She has more or less wiped away the vomit from her hand and mouth. When Darlene comes back, smoking a cigarette, Cheryl says, "You won't believe who was here while you were gone."

"Dean?" Darlene says.

"And Scott. And Brad."

"Brad," the two giggle together. "Do you want a drag?" Darlene says. "It's menthol."

"Do you have a place to sleep tonight?" I ask.

"We don't know where we're going to go," Darlene answers. "We can't go back to Covenant House because we got kicked out. Cheryl got kicked out because they thought she had hash on her. But it wasn't hash, it was Silly Putty."

"Silly Putty?"

"Yes," says Cheryl.

"But they kicked her out anyway. And I had a little knife, it was this big— " and she shows two inches with her fingers. "But they have a rule about no weapons. I would have given it to them if they had told me. So I got kicked out too. Forty-two days before I can go back. I don't know if I'm going to be alive by then." She is working up to a state of hysteria. "I've got no place to stay, and the pimps are waiting for you on the street— "

One of the young men has come back— Brad— and leaning his body close over Cheryl's he puts his face to hers and they talk in whispers.

"Don't you know I love you?" Brad says.

"No."

"No? Why do you say that?"

Darlene says, "I'm going to get Cheryl," apparently meaning some other Cheryl.

"Don't."

Brad suggests to Cheryl that she really did have hash at Covenant House. Darlene gets up. "I'm going to go steal a bag of chips."

"I'll come with you," I say, getting up.

Darlene and I do not steal a bag of chips, but walk down Jarvis Street over to Bond, to see the other Cheryl. Darlene's weaving step makes me concerned that she will step out in front of a car and I occasionally grab her arm. She tells me that she is sixteen, that her father is dead, and that she left her mother in Nova Scotia after being kicked out of school. Her teacher threw a desk at her and in anger Darlene threw back a chair. "I know I shouldn't have thrown that chair, that I just should have walked out of the classroom. But he's still teaching and I'm living on the streets." She tried once to go back to Nova Scotia but says that the drinking there always takes her in. "Okay, I'll admit that I have a drinking problem." But she also says plaintively, "I wish I was with my mother in Nova Scotia right now." She says that her friends mean more to her than she does to herself and that she could not live if anything happened to Cheryl. That's what kids on the street do, she says, they look after one another. Brad is Cheryl's ex-boyfriend and Darlene is hoping that they will get back together. She's sorry they have been kicked out of Covenant House, where she has stayed three or four times, as it's a good place and where she has met many of her friends. When I ask about relatives, she says that she has an uncle who won't take her in, believing her to be a drug addict, and a sister in Oshawa with whom she can't get along. But she does say that more than once her sister has held her up after a drinking bout as she vomited so that she wouldn't choke, saving her life. As we walk I notice that her thin sneakers are soaked through from the earlier rain and her T-shirt too is damp, and she tells me that she is just getting over bronchitis, has athlete's foot, and sclerosis, but of what kind she doesn't say. Instead, her thoughts jump and she tells how on the streets she has seen a guy get stabbed, and another have his legs broken. Again she wonders how she will survive the next forty-two days.

"Did you ever live on the street?" she asks me sincerely.

"No, I never have."

"Well you couldn't have gotten a very good impression from today." She seems embarrassed.

The other Cheryl is living in "sanctuary" in a shelter on Bond Street. That means that while she dries out from liquor and drugs she isn't allowed outside. "She's a dyke, do you know what that means?" Darlene says. "But Cheryl's all right, even though I'm not a dyke, I could never do it with anybody but a man. But Cheryl's just a friend, do you know what I mean? She would never come on to me. She's tough and she looks after us."

I wait inside the door of the shelter as Darlene goes in to talk to Cheryl. I can hear Cheryl telling her that Cheryl-in-the-park will be all right. This Cheryl does look a little tough— a burly girl with short hair, wearing a military cap. But her voice is intelligent and reasonable.

Darlene comes out and we begin to walk again. She tells me that the only possessions she owns are what she has on her and in her little purse. She has no money and no means of getting any. Changing the subject, she tells me how she believes in witchcraft— not in Satan, but in using your will to make things happen. For example, if the government says that twenty thousand people will die in drunk-driving accidents then they will. She also believes that getting hooked on drugs is a matter of will and that's why, despite her occasional use of coke and having freebased five or six times, she won't get addicted. She's sheepish about the drugs, but says they help dull the pain of the street.

At Gerrard and Jarvis we come to a Harvey's and I offer to buy Darlene something to eat. She seems uninterested, but we go inside anyway and Darlene immediately lets out a whoop as she spots three friends. We sit down with them— a young white man, an East Indian woman, and a black woman. "Who's he?" the young man wants to know. He's quite a big guy, wearing a cheap leather jacket with multiple zippers.

I go up to buy a Coke and fries for Darlene. When I sit down again the young man, whose name is Bruce, asks me, "So what are you writing about?"

"I'm writing about how the rich are getting rich and the poor are getting poorer," I say.

"You got it wrong," he says. "It's the rich getting much richer and the poor getting much poorer."

Darlene's mood has completely changed and stretching back her arms, she talks loudly. Spying three policemen at the other side of the restaurant, she says in a bold voice, "I hate cops." And then, even louder, she sings out, "I smell BA—CON!" A couple of people turn their heads and the cops look our way. Bruce takes her by the hand and tells her to calm down. He puts a hand over her mouth. "Take it easy," he says.

"Are you going to order?" says a voice. We turn around to see the manager behind us.

"We're sharing," Darlene says.

"The minimum is a dollar fifty each," the manager says sternly. "Don't you see the sign?" She points.

"Hey, this guy's an author," Bruce says. When that has little effect he sulks, "Okay, we'll go," and he and the two women get up. Outside it has started to pour. "We'll go, too," Darlene says with a sneer. "Only I want some salt first. Four packages."

But Darlene and I don't leave. She puts the salt on the fries and we sit down again, and although the manager stares at us from behind the counter she leaves us alone. Darlene's not very interested in eating the fries and in a few moments four or five more kids come in, followed by Bruce. Darlene springs up and huddles with several other girls by the washrooms, just like girls in high school. Bruce is soaking wet from the rain but seems only amused by it and he comes to sit beside me. Surprisingly, the manager leaves us alone although nobody has ordered any more. "Don't worry about being deserted," he says, nodding towards Darlene. "It happens all the time." Bruce takes from his jacket pocket his birth certificate, his only identification, and finds that it is sopping. He gives it to another friend, a silent Asian boy, to dry in a paper napkin.

Darlene and some of the others come to sit by us. I'm surprised at how they all know one another. She is flying now and her voice is loud as she begins making her anti-cop remarks, only to be disappointed when she sees the police have left. "Chill out," the Asian boy tells her, and he and Bruce try to get her to quieten down. Finally, Bruce, after giving me a pat on the back, takes her outside to give her a talking to.

When she comes back in, Darlene sits with another group of friends and I go over to give her the remainder of the fries (they've been passed around) and her purse.

"Is this the guy in the park?" a girl says. It's Cheryl, whom I would not have recognized, she looks so much younger and sweeter than she had lying on her stomach.

"Don't you recognize me?" I joke.

"I never even saw your face," she smiles shyly.

I stand amazed at how quickly and eagerly they accept a person as a friend, though there's no basis for it, no common background, and not a word about seeing me again. They seem to absorb good will the way children do love. No doubt they have told a few lies, or exaggerated; but how likeable they are. And how remarkable that just two or three hours before the city had seemed impenetrable to me. And it wasn't at all. All I had to do was turn around.

"See you," I say to Darlene. She seems calmer now and happy and there appears to be no concern about where she will sleep tonight. She holds out her small hand to me and luckily I have been observing closely the way they all shake. We do the three deft movements and she gives me a charming, laughing smile.

I walk down Gerrard Street. Looking up, I notice a policeman standing on the sidewalk, one who was in the Harvey's. He stares at me as I go by, not angrily, but curiously.

THE TEN FINALISTS of this year's Miss Toronto pageant are posing in the back of a white Mustang convertible, courtesy of a local car dealership. As a two-man band of off-duty police officers plays rock-gospel music from the stage in Nathan Phillips Square, the young women show off their model training for the photographers— not just the press, but ordinary people, too, and tourists with their automatic cameras.

The Miss Toronto pageant started in 1926, when the Sunnyside Bathing Pavillion was looking for a way to bring in more customers. In 1937 the police department took it over to use as a vehicle for public relations. The ten young women in the back of the Mustang smile and freeze to the click-click-click of the cameras. This has the air of some small-town event, as if time has stood still. And it is how some would like to see the city's daughters: pictures of budding womanhood, safe under a policeman's gaze.

A movement exists to end the Miss Toronto pageant, or at the least to ban beauty contests from city hall. The government, these people argue, should not be party to old-fashioned sexism. But watching these young women posing, I cannot help thinking of Darlene— that she tells us much more about our city than these ten women.

Click-click-click go the cameras.

Singers on a Bus

"WHAT DO WE MEAN by sexual energy?" Stephen Yarmus is saying, holding out his swan-like hands, his long feet curled round the legs of the chair. Stephen is dressed in sweatshirt and cotton pants of the palest blue, the colour that angels might wear should they come down to earth.

"What it means to one of us may not be the same as what it means to another. It may mean simple intercourse or something more. So what does it mean to you?"

A woman in a denim dress says, "It's like— everything. Creativity. Growth. All that."

"That's right," says a young woman. She's smiling but there's an air of unhappiness about her. "It's the universe. But most men— hey, this is my own thing, don't get me started— they don't know that. To them it's okay just to have sex and forget about it."

"But what is sex?" Stephen says, gliding his hands out and then back to his narrow body. "It is a release. Everything is energy and energy builds up in us and must be let go. And so we release it. That's healthy. I don't agree with some yogis who become celibate. That's belief, not understanding. It causes all kinds of neuroses and psychoses. But at the same time, what are the moments when we are most susceptible to having a relationship?"

An older woman says: "When we're lonely."

"The problem is there is too much intellectualizing," says a man with a pot belly and a red face. "It's like going to a cooking class where there isn't any food. I can write poetry or play my guitar and then make love. Without guilt. I mean, who are we condemning here?"

"I hope we're not condemning anybody," says Stephen. "If everyone wants to have an orgy, that's fine." Everyone titters, except for a young man in a tie sitting on the edge of his chair, a thin line of sweat on his lip. What wounds bring them to this skylit room below Dupont Street, to speak of intimate matters before strangers? The young woman might burst into tears, the man in the tie jump up shouting, the red-faced man speak to hear the sound of his own voice in a room of people. Painful and ordinary wounds of the city.

"After sex we are not renewed but are weakened," Stephen bobs forward. "It's an egoic experience. So why are we obsessed with the pursuit of it? Because for that one brief moment of sexual orgasm we surrender our selves to bliss. Enlightenment. But we see just a glimpse. If we could really become enlightened wouldn't it be the experience of bliss all the time? A sort of constant head orgasm?"

BEHIND THE 519 Church Community Centre is Cawthra Park, no more than a green square with a fenced-in wading pool, a small playground, and a slight hill on the north side. On the hill a half-dozen men in bikinis are languorously sunbathing, their bronze chests glistening with suntan oil. The park is small but it is a pleasant and safe oasis where the nearby traffic is only a distant rumble. The men treat the park like a communal back yard.

From the east side of the park comes Jennifer, pushing Ezra in the stroller while Josh peddles his tricycle behind. We enter the wading pool area, where mothers can more easily watch their children, and sit in the shade of a tree. When I talked to Jennifer on the phone she had been depressed; Josh had spat at the babysitter. But today she is bubbling with excitement; the non-profit housing group that she's involved in has just received approval of provincial and federal funds. The group will build over a hundred and twenty-five affordable apartments at Broadview and Danforth.

Someone waves from the other side of the park as a blond woman and an even blonder boy approach, the woman carrying a basket of toys. Jennifer introduces Cynthia, who is twenty-seven and her friend for the past eleven years. Cynthia is not only a working mother but has managed to earn a degree in political science. "Jennifer and I have dumped on each other a lot," Cynthia says, unpacking toys for her five-year-old son, Hugh, to play with. "When Jennifer needs a quiet place just for a cup of tea she comes over." She tells Jennifer how the last time she came to the park some scruffy man let his dog splash around in the wading pool and as the lifeguard did nothing about it Cynthia herself waded in, grabbed the dog by the collar, and trotted it out of the fenced-in area. The dog's owner began to swear and said to her (she imitates an ignorant voice), "Don't your mother learn you no brains?" Jennifer and Cynthia laugh over that, but I am impressed by their proprietary sense of the park and their willingness to enforce its rules to keep the park safe for their children.

As Cynthia buckles on Hugh's roller skates she tells me of her childhood in Niagara-on-the-Lake. Growing up, Cynthia had a big house and yard and a comfortable family of "good Christians." I ask if she had been the family rebel. "Yup," she nods. "I was their brilliant daughter on her way to law school. I would have been twenty-two when I was articling. But I wanted to go to school for the wrong reasons then. I was a clever girl," she laughs, tossing her head back. "And then I ran away to the big city."

Cynthia makes Hugh put on a hockey helmet before he starts roller skating. "Scraped knees will heal, sweety, but heads won't."

As soon as she could after Hugh was born, Cynthia went back to work. When he was ten months old, she began commuting to St. Catharines to take a degree at Brock University, supporting the three of them (Hugh's father had quite his job) by working nights as a bartender in an upscale Rosedale bar and taking out student loans. She graduated despite her common-law husband's antagonism. "He called it my fucking degree from Cow College. Basically it was like that for three years. I worked nights and in the summers. I had to do the cooking, the cleaning, and the laundry. He did nothing."

"There are a lot of guys like that, you know," Jennifer says. "The women do ninety-five percent of the work."

"The other students considered me very radical." Cynthia rolls her eyes. "Because I talked about human rights and individual dignity. So they passed me off as some sort of Commie dyke. They kept telling me that everyone has an equal opportunity in this country! They all wanted to become politicians or work in the civil service, because politics is power." But Cynthia remembers fondly one professor, a Yugoslavian immigrant who loved Canada and appreciated the country's freedoms. When I note that some activists are completely cynical about the country, Cynthia says, "I'd rather be here than the States."

"Yeah," Jennifer says. "That's unrealistic of those people."

And in agreeing, Jennifer mentions in an off-hand manner that she was once in a shelter for battered woman. She hadn't told me that before.

"What I really want to do is go to law school," Cynthia continues. "But it's going to cost so much money, forty thousand dollars in loans and my debt is already eighteen thousand. At Brock I got an eighty percent average with a baby at one breast, a job, and an emotional nightmare. But here I am, not able to go back to school, not paying back my loans yet, and still living in a tiny apartment."

About a year ago Cynthia separated from Hugh's father, but now they are back together again, and I ask if Hugh has suffered from Cynthia's difficulties. "He probably suffered by commuting and the family strain," she considers. "But he's a fairly well adjusted kid. He always has clean clothes, always has medicine when he's sick. If that means my rent is two weeks late so be it. I know what the law is and I'm prepared to use it. And luckily I have a large family. I didn't have to buy him clothes for his first two years." Did Cynthia get back with her husband for the sake of Hugh? "Yeah, probably," she shrugs. "He wasn't always the kind of unsupportive person he got to be. But now everything's great."

"It's about time," says Jennifer, and begins to pack up so that she can pick up her other two kids. Hugh wants a cookie from the community centre's café and as he's too shy to buy it himself Cynthia takes him. Waiting under the tree, I watch some babies in diapers playing in the wading pool while their mothers stand at the edge. A woman with a Spanish accent says, "I don't know the English," and touches her child's bare stomach.

"Navel," another mother instructs her.

"Nahvo," she repeats.

Cynthia and Hugh return and start to play badminton with racquets and birdy from the basket of toys. "I like the neighbourhood and all the shopkeepers around here know me, Cynthia says, "Really, sometimes it feels like a small town. But our cheap apartment is the last of its kind. I'd have to triple my rent just to pay for a better one. Hugh's room is made from a corner of the living room. It's more like a fort. I think, is this the way I want to raise a kid? I'd like to have a yard and a garden. Kids ought to watch things grow. I'd like to have ten kids. But where would I put another one to sleep, in the bathroom? That pisses me off, having my destiny controlled."

Hugh becomes frustrated at missing the birdy and tosses his racquet in frustration. Cynthia takes him gently by the shoulders and gives him a little talking to. He's an easily lovable kid. The afternoon is waning and we pack the toys into the basket. Before she goes, Cynthia wants to tell a final story. Not long ago, when she was working in a Rosedale bar, her second-hand bike was stolen from the front of her apartment building. That bike was Cynthia's major form of transportation and she was furious. "I mean, it had a child's seat on it, for God's sake!" She went to work that night, still upset, and when two women regulars asked her how she was doing, Cynthia poured out her anger. A short time later the two women went around the tables and within five minutes gathered five hundred dollars. Triumphantly they presented the money to Cynthia. "I felt shitty, just rotten," Cynthia says. "That wasn't why I told them. I didn't want to become a game— how much can you pressure people into coughing up? Somebody puts in fifty because his friend only put in twenty. I have some pride. So I tried to give the money back. Three times, but nobody would tell me how much they gave."

One of the women who had passed the hat told Cynthia that she had done it because her own two-year-old child had drowned in their swimming pool; the nanny hadn't pulled her out in time. "Like it wasn't for me— it was for her she was doing this. She said that these people have more money than they know what to do with. So I took the money home. And the next day the owner found out. He accused me of taking advantage of the job and equated me with another waitress who had begun dating customers and accepting gifts from some of the married men. So I kept being insulted— first by the theft, then by the women, and finally by the owner. That's what happens when you don't have any money."

"Let's go, sweetheart," she says, swinging Hugh in her arms so that he giggles uncontrollably. And what happened to the money?

"Well," she smiles. "I got a new bike."

THE MAIN ROAD of High Park divides the formal garden entrance to run gently down the sloping decline of the park. On a bench a woman wrapped in a shawl is speaking in Hungarian to her companion beneath the branches of a tremendous oak tree. Old men in hats— straw hats, felt and cloth hats— occupy the picnic tables, throwing down cards. And on the tables, piles of one and two dollar bills. They might be the same old men who played here when I was a child, as if the world hadn't changed at all.

At the playground, fathers are pulling the shirts off their children's thin bodies to send them shrieking into the wading pool. Young men on racing bikes chat in Italian as they glide by. I follow the murky stream, down a descending series of miniature waterfalls to Grenadier Pond. Four boys are fishing off the dock, and one of them whistles as the little trolly-train trundles by, the conductor ringing the bell. I sit down on a bench facing the water.

Earlier in the day I had met with Elizabeth Amer, the city councillor, and we walked together from City Hall to a Queen Street café called Express, with black minimalist chairs and cork-coloured tables. I had known Liz for several years, ever since we worked together as editorial staff on *The Canadian Forum*. Back then she was the spokesperson for the residents of Ward's Island, whom the Metro government was trying to evict from their cottage-like houses, and at each new crisis the office would be flooded with reporters and television cameras. Liz would give them her statement, but it was clear that she felt uncomfortable in the limelight. That's why I was surprised to hear that she was running in the last election for the New Democratic Party. Since the election, Liz's voting record has earned her the title of best newcomer to city council by Reform Toronto, and journalists have praised her reform stance. There has also been criticism of Liz as a politician, both in public and private. But I wanted to talk to Liz to find out what it felt like to be on the other side. And to ask how she could make decisions that would affect a city and the people in it. For Liz was never ashamed to admit that there were many things she didn't understand, or to show confusion in the face of a complex issue, the sort of confusion that causes many of us to leave these decisions in the hands of others.

Over lunch, Liz said that she always knew she would run for council after her children were grown, and that in the last few months she had moved from an almost exclusively domestic life to an equally exclusively public one. And although she infuriated her fellow NDP members on council by refusing to attend ribbon-cutting ceremonies and ethnic functions, she still found the work almost overwhelming. "The greatest surprise was the sheer volume of material that has to be processed," she said. "The number of decisions we have to make is astounding. Yesterday a hundred and eighty-three items were on the agenda— that means a hundred and eighty-three decisions. I'm not interested in being an umpire for the allocation of private property rights— which of the property interests is going to get rich. That's land use and it takes up most of our time. I have a whole different agenda, which is to make sure that the city's services are really available to the lower income people who need them. I want the city to be rich, because then theoretically the resources for people will be there. Some people think you can get public benefit out of working with developers and making deals, but I've found it very difficult. Where is the benefit for the people on the lower level of the income scale?"

I told Liz of my meeting with Allan Blott, the development lawyer, and what he said about developers needing to be patient because city councils don't last. "It's true," she said, "developers and the city bureaucracy remain." She told me of a meeting she had had just that morning with a representative from the Harbour Castle Hotel and from the Toronto Transit Commission. Both groups want to build an underground tunnel from the new Light Rapid Transit station at Bay and Queen's Quay into the Harbour Castle, adding to the already extensive underground network that connects the downtown. But Liz was against the hotel paying part of the cost.

"To me this is a movement towards the privatization of the TTC," she said. "The stop is already called the Harbour Castle. Why name a public transit stop after a private corporation? The tunnel wouldn't be wheelchair accessible and I don't think the city should build any public transit that isn't. And it isn't really public because of the tight security at Harbour Castle. They don't want people pouring from the LRT into their hotel. There's another reason, too. Jane Jacobs wrote that for city streets to be safe there must be people on them, coming and going at all hours. Putting people underground drains the streets of those people. It drains the city of life."

Liz wanted to talk not about her own positions, but about creating opposition. "The government comes to me when it wants to know what Ward Five is thinking," she said. "I'm Ward Five. But the truth is only a small percentage of the people in the ward actually voted for me. And how do you know what people want, phone a few at random? So I'm trying to organize groups in the ward— groups that already exist— to tell me what they think and what they want." As Liz is an endorser of Bread Not Circuses, I brought it up as an an example of an opposition group trying to get funding from the city. Liz readily agreed that the money was necessary. "There are eight thousand people working for the city. How many people are working for Bread Not Circuses?" A handful of volunteers and community workers, I said. "Well, if you do a power analysis of that contest you can see that it isn't very equal. The question is, how do they enhance their power and diminish ours?"

Now, in High Park, the boys on the dock throw out their fishing lines again. I get up from the bench and walk down to Colborne Lodge, the house of John George Howard, who gave his land to the city in 1873 to form the basis of the park. An architect, Howard laid the first sidewalk on King Street— twelve-inch wooden planks, two wide. The road back winds past the tennis courts and the swimming pool and, down below, the deer pens that I had forgotten since childhood.

Past the Grenadier Restaurant, in a clearing of grass and gnarled trees where a few sunbathers lie with their bathing straps undone, stands a bronze statue. Like most of the city's public art, the statue is a mediocre one, a stiff and formal figure rising larger than life and dressed in vaguely classical robes. Its profile is of an idealized and cooly beautiful woman. Against the base leans a wreath of flowers that looks wilted despite being artificial. On the pedestal is chiselled the name of the figure, Lesya Ukrainka, and the information that she is THE GREATEST UKRAINIAN POETESS. And two lines of her poetry.

BY MY OWN HANDS FREEDOM GAINED IS FREEDOM TRUE
BY OTHERS FREEDOM GIVEN IS A CAPTIVE'S DOOM

As poetry the lines are bad, and they ring with the sort of nationalist rhetoric that always makes me uneasy. Yet I think I know what Lesya Ukrainka meant, and an image comes to me of that man with the guitar who was the only one not to applaud when the politician stepped forward. Because he knew where his own freedom came from.

I know that just taking that first step out of privacy and silence is a healing, a liberating act. I've seen it in others and I begin to see it in myself. But that may not be enough to save a city, or make it what it has never yet been. And it's naive to believe that all of us are equally free to speak, that one voice, even if whispered, won't be privileged over another. Still, if I haven't found absolute conviction, or even an ending, I have found a revelation of sorts, and it seems somehow fitting that it should come from bad poetry on a public statue.

THE MEMBERS of the Bread Not Circuses Coalition are sitting in a ragged circle in the room just outside the chapel of the church in Regent Park, a breeze coming through the tilted windows. Most of those present represent a member-group of the coalition such as Women Plan Toronto or St. Christopher House, but some, like Parika, are here on their own.

During one of the reports, someone leans into the room to say that Ringo, an occasional attendant at the meetings, is having a fit. Two people immediately rush out, including a nurse, and the meeting continues. Some time later Ringo reappears, looking a little sheepish as he hangs about the doorway.

A lot of time is spent evaluating the people's cultural festival that was held in Queen's Park. The turnout was a disappointment but everyone agrees that the spirit of the festival was high and the media coverage was good. I pipe up to say that while the turnout might have been small, polls show that many people in the city have the same concerns that we do. A couple of people nod vigorously and, though I know it's rather foolish, I feel suddenly good, for this is the first time I have spoken at a meeting. For now on when I attend it will be as a participant and not as an observer.

Several new ideas are voiced over the evening: a banner for the labour day parade, a street opera. The whole meeting is positive and energetic and I find myself feeling strangely happy. At the close we all get up but instead of rushing off, everyone lingers to talk. Ringo is back in the room now, a big fellow with jet black hair, a deep voice and an impressively large nose. He tells me that during his epileptic seizure he got "ripped off" but it takes me a moment to understand; while he was writhing on the floor a man removed his watch and a packet of cigarettes. That a person can rob another when he is defenceless is so appalling I don't know what to say. Ringo's voice sounds hurt but resigned. "At least he didn't take this," he says, pulling from beneath his shirt a simple cross on a chain. "A friend who passed away gave this to me. It has memories."

Parika and I step down into the night and head to George's for a Coke. Parika rubs her eyes with fatigue, but as usual she inundates me with her thoughts on half a dozen meetings and issues. Not long ago she was banned from Dufferin Mall. "I was just sitting there, reading the newspaper. And a guard came up and told me to leave. I thought he was joking, I didn't even know they had the power to do that. So I ignored him. And then he asked me to come to the office where he gave me a piece of paper that said I was barred."

But Parika refuses to be passive; she has gone to a legal-aid clinic to help her fight the order. She tells me of a proposed bill that will give people more rights in malls, recognizing them as public places. Tells me, even though she is so tired that her head droops as she walks along the street that is dark but for streaks of neon.

OUTSIDE THE BUS bus window, Bay Street is dark and almost deserted. The bus itself is overly lit, and, tired, I lean my head back and close my eyes. For a moment I imagine that I am dreaming, for a sound is filling the bus, a sweet harmony of voices. I turn around to see five young black men sitting at the back, neatly dressed in cardigans and jackets, and while one snaps his fingers for rhythm they sing together, one of those crossover songs that can be about the love of God or a girl, or even a city if you should choose. On they sing, as the bright bus glides through the night. Wanting to share this moment, I look from one passenger to another, but the few on the bus stare unsmiling into the dark, as if they did not hear the music, as if there were no music. How disappointing, and how typical of Toronto! Then, just behind me, yes, there is a person smiling, an elderly and dignified woman. It takes me a moment to recognize her as the woman I spoke to on the bench in Parkdale, the woman who had come down to heal our wounds. Mrs. God. She hears the music and she is smiling.